STUDENT LIFE:

Letters and Recollections

FOR A YOUNG FRIEND.

By SAMUEL OSGOOD,

AUTHOR OF

"Studies in Biography," "The Hearth-Stone," "Mile-Stones," &c,

Ne certés can that Friendship long endure,
However gay and goodly be the style,
That doth ill cause or evill end enure,
For Vertue is the band that bindeth Harts most sure.

SPENSER.

NEW YORK:
JAMES MILLER, 554 BROADWAY.
1861.

Entered according to Act of Congress in the year 1860, by
JAMES MILLER,
In the Clerk's Office of the District Court of the United States, for the Southern District of New York.

R. CRAIGHEAD,
Printer, Stereotyper, and Electrotyper,
Caxton Building,
81, 83, *and* 85 *Centre Street.*

To

PRESIDENT QUINCY,

BY

ONE OF THE CLASS OF 1832.

CONTENTS.

PREFACE.

A FRIEND, whofe fon had juft entered college a few months ago, afked for him a word of counfel from the author, and a single offhand letter was written accordingly. The friend, and alfo the fon, fuggefted that fome more letters would be welcome, and that good would furely be done by printing them. Six letters were foon written, and thefe, with revifion and the addition of a few thoughts and recollections, are now publifhed in this little volume.

Thus, without any intention on his own part, the author finds his name once more on a title page, quite willing to follow the advifers, young and old, who afk for this publication, and who affure him that it will be ufeful; quite certain, moreover, that he has written to meet an aƈtual want, and with the ſimple purpoſe of ſaying a kind and true word to ſtudents in loving remembrance of old college days. The author's ſympathies, like his perſonal experience, are cloſely with thoſe who are obliged to depend upon themſelves; and there may be ſome words here that will encourage young perſons, without fortune and even without parents or patrons, to preſs on in a worthy career with ſtrength and hope.

It ſeemed beſt to retain the dates and names, generally, as they originally ſtood, and if this feature gives the book more of a Cambridge air, it will be more expreſſive, even to general readers, than if the thought were purely imperſonal, without local habitation or name. The contents are ſomewhat deſultory, but they all bear upon the title and illuſtrate ſome aſpects of Student Life.

The author is grateful to his friend and claſsmate, Rev. Charles T. Brooks, for the fine poem at the "Silver Feſtival." If the bulk of the book were but earth, this roſe, like that of Saadi's Guliſtan, would be enough to ſweeten the whole lump.

New York, Nov. 28, 1860.

STUDENT LIFE.

I.

GENERAL IDEAS OF STUDY.

DEAR ——, I propofe, in a very familiar manner, to give you the refults of my own experience in college, looked back upon from nearly thirty years' experience of life.

You go to college to get an education; and, of courfe, ftudy is the main intereft of the next four years. It is marvellous how much can be learned in that fhort period, with due diligence and economy of time. The firft thing for you to do will be to make the beft divifion poffible of the hours of the day, fo as to eftablifh a good working method, that will harmonize the claims of different ſtudies with each other, and all ſtudies with proper reſt and recreation. The college leſſons ſettle the quantity to be learned each day, but the mode of learning will be left very much to you, and you will gain much in ſpirits and time by a due alternation of ſtudies, ſuch as following mathematics by language, or varying the poſture of the mind by wiſe alternation between ſubjects that ſtrain and concentrate the attention, and thoſe that pleaſantly move the fancy or poſſess the memory. I have often found, for example, that after I have wearied myſelf over hard problems in calculus or geometry, it is almoſt play to read a chapter of a Latin hiſtorian or an Engliſh moraliſt or metaphyſician. The mind, like the body, ſeems to have two legs, and is ſoon weary of ſtanding wholly on one of them.

As to the relative importance of ſtudies, you will have frequent deciſions to make, not only in chooſing voluntaries, but in the amount of time and attention to be given to the requiſite branches of the regular courſe. The moſt comprehenſive diviſion is between what may be called ſtudies of *ſequence*, or ſuch as carry out a continuous thread of thought—ſuch as mathematics, grammar, philoſophy—and ſtudies of *aggregation*, or ſuch as merely add to the ſtock of learning—ſuch as additional claſſic authors, or modern languages. To omit ſome of the latter may only leſſen your ſtock of learning, whilſt to neglect the former is to mutilate your whole education, break the line of ſtudy, and even impair your powers of thinking. Studies of ſequence are like the bolts that faſten the train of cars to the engine, whilſt ſtudies of aggregation are like the baggage which is to be taken on board, and which, however important, is not abſolutely eſſential to a ſafe paſſage.

After maſtering the eſſential ſtudies, you will have ſome time to ſpare for voluntary branches, and I adviſe you to give the modern languages the preference over *belles lettres*, becauſe in youth we are more capable of learning languages, and the rudiments of grammar and accent if then acquired never leave us, whilſt ſtudies of taſte, ſuch as biography, poetry, reviews, eſſays, and even hiſtory, can be as well attended to afterwards, when the reflective powers are matured. Among modern languages, I regard French and German eſſential, and Italian and Spaniſh very deſirable for you.

You will remember, however, that it is more important to learn *language* than languages; and the acquiſition of various languages is chiefly important becauſe it gives us ſuch command of our own. Thus, the beſt exerciſe in Engliſh diction to a beginner is the exact and elegant tranſlation of a foreign author. I uſed, beſides learning my Latin leſſons in a general way, to ſtudy a certain portion, ſay a page, very carefully, ſo as to give to each word and idiom the juſt, and if poſſible the elegant rendering. A page of Livy or Tacitus thus ſtudied will teach you more and better Engliſh than a dozen themes on the hackneyed ſubjects of an abſtract kind, ſuch as uſually vex the brain of beginners in compoſition. Study language in this way, and you will find theme-writing much eaſier; and when, moreover, you come to practiſe extempore ſpeaking, as you muſt ſoon do, you will find a claſſic vocabulary riſing to your lips in a manner that will often ſurpriſe you.

I might ſay much more upon your future ſtudies, but I muſt paſs on to ſpeak of your ſtudent character. Vices I do not warn you againſt, and I will not caution you againſt exceſſes that would break the heart of your father and mother, as well as contradict all your own promiſe and diſpoſition. But you are expoſed to the prevailing infirmity of young men, eſpecially of well-to-do families—the danger of leaving ſtern duties very much to themſelves, and of drifting through college without honor and without ſhame, in an eaſy, inefficient way, that may leave you a dainty gentleman, but cannot make you a good ſcholar or a true man. You will be likely very ſoon to form deciſive habits, ſuch as virtually decide your college career, by ſetting the mark in your own mind, and creating a very powerful expectation in the minds of thoſe who know you. Look well to this, and let a true and brave purpoſe to be faithful to your own mind, to your family, and to God, begin with your beginning, and go with you to the end.

Companions are great elements in a ſtudent's career, and it is hard to be right without right ſympathy and coöperation. You ſeem to be of a ſympathetic and ſuſceptible nature, and your force will depend very much upon your aſſociates. You muſt be courteous and even friendly to all; but you can have but few intimates, and let theſe be thoſe who help your beſt purpoſes. If I were to chooſe two neareſt companions for a ſon, one ſhould be a ſuperior whom he could follow, and the other ſhould be an equally congenial inferior whom he could lead; for it is as eſſential to true companionſhip that we give worthy influence as well as receive it, and ſociety is moſt complete when it invites us to be both maſter and diſciple. Watch your opportunity, and you will find fit companions, though, perhaps, few; and in their ſympathy you will find it eaſy to withſtand a falſe and tyrannical public opinion, ſuch as frequently prevails in a claſs, and to take and keep the poſition that beſt ſecures your own honor, and in the end commands the reſpect of all.

God's bleſſing be upon you, dear ——. May life and health be granted you to finiſh your courſe well. Be a good ſcholar, a pure, and faithful, and brave ſpirit; and whilſt ſhining gifts may develop themſelves in your career, you will be ſure to be a bleſſing to your family and kindred, and an honor to the Alma Mater whoſe loyal ſons it is your father's great comfort and mine to be.

Yours, affectionately,

—— ——.

II

COLLEGE RANK.

I TAKE your ſuggeſtion readily, my dear friend, and am glad to add a few words of advice upon ſome of the moſt important points in your univerſity career, after ſpeaking as I did in my firſt letter of the general principles to be borne in mind. There is no more conſpicuous and important point to be conſidered than that of college rank. The moment you join your claſſmates, you will hear the queſtion aſked, "Who is to be our firſt ſcholar?" and each of the four years will give new intereſt to the queſtion; whilſt, perhaps, as long as you live, you will remember the order in which your fellows ſtood on the liſt, and it will not be eaſy to believe that thoſe old diſtinctions can be ever done away.

Let us underſtand what we mean by college rank, and try to make a due eſtimate of its importance as a motive. It means not, in general, the rank which a ftudent wins in college as a perfon of honor and efficiency among his companions and teachers, but that which he holds upon the fcale of merit which is formed from the fum total of marks made by teachers in the recitation-room, and which is not ufually modified by confiderations of perfonal character, unlefs an afpirant's virtues are fo positive as to quicken and exalt his intellect, or unlefs his faults are fo ftrong as to fhow themfelves in open indolence or vice. It is evident, then, that whilft this fcale of merit decides much in a ftudent's career, yet it does not decide all; and he may have much good or evil, wifdom or folly, in his mind and ways, which is not marked upon the lift, fo that fome ftudents from their average scholarfhip ftand well on the books who ftand ill with the clafs; and others, who from efpecial talents and purfuits or characteriftics ftand well with the clafs, ftand ill on the books. In faying this, we are only faying that the college regifter is not infallible, and that the diftribution of academic honors is not the act of the final and fupreme Judge. The decifion is very important, as giving a generally important and reafonably approximate view of the ufe that ftudents have made of their time and powers. It is the beſt *outward* criterion that can be appealed to, much ſafer than claſs opinion, since claſs popularity depends, eſpecially at firſt, upon very uncertain qualities; and the daſhing youth who is ſo full of generous impulſes as to ſlur the ſelf-denying virtues, and ſo ſtrong in native talent or early training as to deſpiſe plodding induſtry, is moſt likely to be the favorite of the majority, eſpecially of the numerous hoſt of idlers and free-and-eaſy fellows, who like a brilliant companion and apologiſt in their own ſhortcomings.

I adviſe you to pay great reſpect to the ſcale of merit—not, indeed, as the ſupreme rule, or the higheſt good, but as a very valuable record of what you are doing, and ſignificant reminder of what you ought to do. I know that ſome perſons profeſs to deſpiſe college rank as a mean conſideration, and others to condemn it as demoralizing. But ſurely it is not mean to wiſh to know how we are purſuing our ſtudies in compariſon with others, nor is it demoralizing to try to do as well as we can in competition with them. The principle of emulation or rivalry, indeed, as the main motive to ſtudy, is a very imperfect and objectionable one; yet we muſt remember that if ſome perſons are *above* the ſpirit of rivalry, others are *below* it; and it is far better that a youth ſhould ſtart bravely on his career under the ſpur of competition, than that he ſhould not ſtart at all, but ſhould be found ſtagnating in lazineſs and ignorance, whilſt his companions are preſſing on in a race which wakes nobler powers and aſpirations than were felt at the outſet. Much as may be ſaid againſt emulation, it is certain that it cannot wholly be diſmiſſed, and that our ſocial nature is ſuch that it is very hard if not impoſſible to think only of abſolute and ideal excellence, and even the moſt ſaintly characters, who have riſen above all petty rivalry, are vaſtly ſtimulated to new efforts by each other's virtues, like the Apoſtle, who would have his friends conſider each other, and "provoke to love and good works."

Let me be diſtinctly underſtood as to the juſt uſe of the principle of emulation. It would certainly taint your affections at once, if you entered the field ſolely or mainly to diſtance your rival or rivals, for you thus ſubordinate the purſuit of knowledge and the diſcipline of the faculties to perſonal competition, and ſucceſs itſelf becomes morally defeat, whilſt defeat becomes doubly ſuch, and wrecks pride and principle at once. Yet, if you ſay that you will never care how you ſtand in the general average, you deceive yourſelf, for you do care; and the very ſtudents who affect moſt to deſpiſe college rank, are very emulous for other things—emulous to be firſt on the liſt of dainty gentlemen, or renowning bullies, leaders of the roughs or the ſmooths, the hards or the ſofts, those laſting diſtinctions that divide the idlers of the claſs. The feeling againſt thoſe who think mainly of winning a high rank is very ſtrong, not only among the idlers, but the generous and manly portion of the claſs; yet it is directed, not againſt thoſe who wiſh to ſtand well, but againſt thoſe who are aiming conſtantly to ſtand better than others, and who tend to carry rivalry to the extreme of envy, if not detraction. Erring as claſs-opinion is apt to be, it has no ſtigma for thoſe who are willing to have it fully underſtood that they came to college to ſtudy, and they wiſh to have a free field and fair play, with as much ſucceſs aſcribed to them as they win, and no more.

I adviſe you to act ſomewhat in this wiſe in reſpect to college honors. Make as fair an eſtimate as you can of your talents and acquiſitions, to begin with. You will carry to college with you ſome definite opinion of what you are, and what you can do. As you, my dear fellow, entered, I am glad to hear, without any conditions, this fact proves that you have at leaſt fair gifts, and that you ought to ſtand well in your claſs. It is ample proof that you can begin with good hope the ſtudies of your courſe. Learn every leſſon well, and as new branches taſk new faculties, and you come into competition with your claſſmates, you can form a ſomewhat poſitive eſtimate of what your juſt level is, or the place that you can win and keep by proper method and exertion. You may find yourſelf perhaps eaſily or decidedly at the head of your claſs the firſt term. If this is ſo, you ought not to loſe your place by indolence or negligence, and whilſt fidelity to all your opportunities is the higheſt rule of action, this rule will not be ſet aſide, but may be ſtrengthened by a fair ſtatement of your progreſs, such as your teachers can give you. The ſcale of rank will then be, not your guiding motive, but your time-keeper—not, indeed, ſtarting you on your journey, but adviſing you whether you have kept your way with due diligence. In ſome caſes a youth who ſtarts as the firſt ſcholar muſt inevitably reſign his place to ſome competitor who ſurpaſſes him in the later ſtudies, ſuch as the higher mathematics, metaphyſics, and original thinking and compoſition. In ſuch caſe it becomes the diſappointed one to meaſure his dignity by fidelity, not by victory, and zealouſly—nay, devoutly—beware of ſo ſetting his heart upon ſurpaſſing a rival as to meaſure the ſucceſs of his career by a ſtandard ſadly embittering and demoralizing. The great aim ſhould be to find out our own orbit, and move in it ſaithfully, whatever it may be.

In a large number of a claſs like yours, of over a hundred members, there muſt be defects of native endowment, and a conſiderable proportion muſt have very limited talents, ſo that nothing can be more fooliſh than for parents to exact of a ſon the very higheſt reſults, without reſpect to native gifts. It is cruel to tell a youth to be firſt ſcholar at any rate, becauſe he may not have ſufficient talent, or elſe he may have ſuch peculiar talents that the higheſt fidelity to his own mind may not allow him to give ſuch time and thought to all the branches of ſtudy as to win the palm in all. Making all fair allowance, however, for difference of talent, it is obvious that the moſt marked cauſe of defective ſcholarſhip is negligence, and that an induſtrious youth of determined induſtry and moderate gifts may depend upon bearing a reſpectable rank, certainly on ſtanding in the firſt quarter of the claſs, and ſecuring a part at commencement. It is equally obvious that a youth of good talents, with due induſtry, may ſtand among the firſt ten or twelve ſcholars.

If I am aſked whether college rank is worth ſtriving for from its promiſe of after efficiency, and whether high ſcholars keep their relative place in the world, I can ſay without qualification, that diſtinction in ſcholarſhip is a certain good, but not always the higheſt good. If you rank as firſt in your claſs at graduating, you carry into the world an amount of knowledge and habits of application that ought to ſerve you through life. Yet no miſtake can be greater than to miſtake the beginning for the end, or to confound, as ſome do, the preparation for the work of life with the work itſelf. Firſt ſcholars often do this, and think that they have hit the mark when they have merely won their way into the arena, fooliſhly aſſuming the airs of conqueſt when they have only learned to uſe their weapons and wear their armor. It is not ſtrange, therefore, that they often yield in the actual world to more determined and leſs ſanguine aſpirants, who go to work as if the battle were to be won, and who juſtify their brave and modeſt purpoſes by ſtout blows and rich trophies. Moreover, high ſcholars are often indebted to ready memory, a glib tongue, and a verſatile mind, for a diſtinction in ſtudy which cannot be kept up when new fields call for ſtern work, and taſk the more aggreſſive and effective powers, eſpecially the powers of original thought, practical judgment, and manly courage. Yet the diſappointment of ſuch ſcholars does not diſparage their induſtry or their rank, but ſimply ſhows that there are different gifts, and whilſt their faithful ſtudy did much for them, it did not do everything. In one reſpect, perhaps, a ſtudent who is bent on winning the higheſt rank may ſometimes damage his efficiency in the world by ſpreading his energies over too wide a ſurface, neglecting the ſpecial gifts which are his peculiar prerogative and main dependence. Yet even here there is a compenſation, ſince the ſtudies which regard for rank moves him to purſue, are thoſe that he may moſt need to complete his culture, whilſt the ſtudies that are his ſpecial branches are pretty ſure to have attention enough without being interfered with by other branches. I believe, however, that high ſcholarſhip, as marked by the ſcale of rank, is an unalloyed good, when ſought and won with true practical aim; and the moſt frequent cauſe of the failure of college rank to keep its place in the world ariſes from the too frequent paſſion for immediate ſucceſs, or the habit of depending on immediate applauſe, as in the recitation-room, inſtead of ſtriving for an object good in itſelf, and looking to a diſtant day to juſtify and reward the ſtriving. I therefore conſider that ſtudent as having the beſt promiſe of uſefulneſs and ſucceſs in life who unites the beſt ſcholarſhip with the moſt practical aims, and who ſtudies for the ſubſtance, not for the ſhow of things. This combination is rarely found very low in the ſcale of rank, and not always at the top of the liſt. If the college catalogue is carefully ſtudied, it will be found, probably, that the moſt effective men have been thoſe who have united a determined purpoſe with fair if not brilliant ſcholarſhip, and the firſt ſcholar by the college ſcale is often if not generally diſtanced by ſome man of more nerve, if of leſs verſatility, in the ſterner arena of life.

Summing up our ideas practically, I advife you to think of college rank, not as the end, but as one of the means of felf-difcipline and manly culture. It will be of great ufe to you if you are apt to be carelefs and languid, drifting with the ftream of events and companions without thinking of the result. It will keep you pofted up as to your actual proficiency, and may fhow you how negligent you have been or are becoming, before you are aware of any change in your method; as fome loiterer who may think he has time enough to ramble in the woods before returning home, finds by a glance at his watch that the hours are paffing, and he muft haften back, or ftumble on the dark mountains. If you do the beft that in you lies, it will be ufeful to know how you ftand in regard to your claffmates, and what ftudies you are thought moft to neglect or leaft able to purfue with efficiency. If, on the contrary, you begin feebly, and are doing little or nothing, it is well for you to know it, and either change your courfe, or elfe leave college at once, inftead of being a ftudent only in name, and fhaming high opportunities by pitiful performance. Be affured that neglect of the regular college ftudies is no light lofs, and that future energy, whilft it may give new wiſdom and power, can never reſtore to you the loſt hours and leſſons of your youth.

One word in concluſion—a word probably more pertinent to your caſe. If you find yourſelf ambitious of diſtinction, and painfully alive to competition, ſtrive to warm and elevate rivalry as much as you can by generous ſympathy and enthuſiaſm. Know and love your competitors, and ſtudy with them, ſo as to try to feel, and make them feel that there is a fellowſhip of purſuits and gifts. If you ſurpaſs them in ſome things, allow that in other things you are ſurpaſſed by them, and thus ſee, and make them ſee, that all ſuperiority has in itſelf a ground of deference and a need of companionſhip. He who bears the palm will then not fail to be modeſt in his triumph, and he who yields it after manly ſtriving will not loſe ſelf-reſpect nor fellow-feeling. Thus emulation, whilſt it keeps its zeſt, will loſe its ſting, and they who have been rivals in rank will be none the leſs friends and helpers in all coming time. Sad and ſometimes terrible is the oppoſite courſe, when rivalry is ſo intenſe and perſonal as to become bitter and even malign, poiſoning the motives of ſtudy, ruining the true qualities of the ſpirit, and bringing the worſt paſſions of the world into the ſacred retreats of letters. Againſt ſuch rivalry ſtrive and pray. May God open to you, as to us in our day, a circle of cheriſhed companions who are near at heart as in ſtudies, and who gain, and continue ſtill to gain from each other far more by mutual encouragement than by jealous competition. It was a priceleſs bleſſing to us, that thoſe who were moſt cloſely rivals by poſition were the cloſeſt friends in affection and principle.

I may write you again on college ſocieties, and ſociety at large.

III.

COMPANIONS AND CLUBS.

I TOUCHED a little in my firſt letter upon college friendſhips, but the ſubject is ſo important as to demand conſideration by itſelf. You already feel as never before the value and ſignificance of aſſociates, in preſence of your hundred claſſmates, who are every day ſurpriſing you with new developments of character, and awakening within you new affinities and antipathies. There is a great deal in your future ſocial career that will take care of itſelf; and when no poſitive principle forbids, it is beſt for a youth to follow the great law of elective affinities, and go moſt with the companions whom he beſt likes, and who beſt like him. Yet his free choice will be pretty ſure to move in paths of ſettled conviction, as well as of pleaſant taſtes, and the ſtronger is his ſenſe of honor and purity, the more ſelect will his aſſociations be. Eſpecially will he be able to exerciſe diſcretion in chooſing between the various college ſocieties that ſolicit his intereſt and participation; and if he may find on his liſt of friends ſome kind-hearted fellow whoſe indolence or laxity he cannot approve, he can have no excuſe for committing himſelf to organized aſſociations that tend to foſter indolence or laxity.

You will find yourſelf buſily ſtudying character around you for ſome months to come, and making eſtimates that further experience will ſometimes fix, and ſometimes wholly ſet aſide. Some who captivate you at firſt ſight by cordial manners and generous ideas, will keep their hold upon you for life, binding you to them with a golden chain that brightens by being worn; whilſt others, perhaps equally attractive at the outſet, will ſoon fail to pleaſe you, as the dull lead or the corroſive braſs ſhows out from under the flaſhy waſh of the ſurface. For a while, the diverſity of traits will seem ſo great as to defy all attempts at claſſification; but before many months have gone—certainly at the cloſe of your firſt year—you will find the crowd indicating certain leading tendencies, as he who watches the waters of a bay ſees in time that what ſeemed an indiſcriminate maſs has its depths, ſhallows, and tides, and that, inſtead of being left to the play of chance, the waters follow certain dominant diſpoſitions, and are likely ſo to do ſo long as ſhores, and winds, and heavens are the ſame.

Perhaps the firſt diſtinction that impreſſes you after the very natural intereſt you muſt take in deciding upon the looks of your claſs, and chatting as uſual upon the candidates for the honors of being the Apollo or the Hercules of your Pantheon, will be made by the apparent diſtinctions of fortune. You muſt obſerve, by the furniture, dreſs, and general habits of ſome, that they have plenty of money to ſpend, whilſt others bear marks of great limitation—a limitation that ſometimes amounts to pinching poverty. Once in a while you may be tempted to ſmile at a claſſmate's coat or pantaloons that may bear marks of having been worn threadbare by ſome elder of the family before ſerving the preſent wearer, and yet you may ſoon find the wearer to be an earneſt, noble fellow, of whoſe acquaintance you are proud, and whoſe mental riches you may covet. Obtruſive as the diſtinction of wealth is at firſt, it holds of itſelf, in the long run, a very ſmall place in college opinion; and many a poor ſtudent who has to work and pinch himſelf to pay his term bills, has a place not only in the recitation-room, but on the College Green, and in the literary and ſocial clubs, that the ſon of the millionaire generally deſpairs of attaining. No aſpect of college life is more grateful to be remembered than the general kindneſs toward thoſe who are ſtruggling with hard fortunes; and I heard this fact commented upon moſt tenderly this very week, by two Cambridge graduates who ſpoke from perſonal experience, and received the higheſt honors of their claſs, after helping themſelves on by making fires, ringing bells, and other honeſt but ſomewhat homely acts of uſefulneſs. I allow that there is a good deal of a certain caſte or ariſtocracy in college, and that much preſtige is given by high family, eſpecially when aſſociated with a noble bearing, and either with a commanding carriage or brilliant talents. The youth who is moſt eaſily the claſs-favorite is he who is at once the genial gentleman and the gifted ſcholar, ſeeming more to prevail by blood and genius than by hard ſtudy, and to ſucceed more becauſe he cannot help it, than becauſe he cares about diſtancing a rival, or ſtanding well upon the rank-liſt. The beſt ſpecimen of this ſtyle of character may, however, have his moſt intimate friend in a ſtudent whoſe pedigree and whoſe purſe are equally ſcanty, and whoſe ſtrong ſenſe and loyal ſtudy enable him to give to his lordlier aſſociate far more than he receives. In fact, no greater bleſsing can happen to a claſs, than when the lords and commons are brought together in generous coöperation under the leaderſhip of two ſuch characters, as when the Cobdens and Ruſſells, or Franklins and Waſhingtons put their heads and hands together, and the people ſay, Amen.

If I were to adviſe a ſon to regulate his conduct at all with reference to diſtinctions of wealth, it would be mainly to warn him againſt the habits of expenſe that are uſually foſtered by the richer ſtudents, and to urge him to live in great ſimplicity, ſuch as leſſens inſtead of widening the line between the rich and the poor in college. Habits of expenſe are likely to nurture a wholly falſe taſte, and lead to the miſerable miſtake of confounding the amount of money ſpent with the amount of good to be received. The beſt ſtandard of living is that which brings a ſtudent near to the common lot, and makes him enter moſt heartily into the feelings of thoſe who have their own way to make in the world, and who eat, and drink, and dreſs, and ſtudy in ſuch a way as beſt to fit them to take a ſolid and independent poſition in the world. The common lot is like the common ſoil, the brown earth on which we tread, and plough, and plant. The ſeed may have a daintier look when wrapped in white paper, and put upon the ſhelf, than when ſown broadcaſt upon the land; but only when taken from the ſhelf, and put into the ground, does it germinate and bear fruit. The youth who goes mainly with the rich or excluſive, miſſes the wholeſome brown earth where growth moſt thrives; and I could not promiſe well of any ſtudent's future who did not have among his intimates ſome hard-working companions from the great middling claſs of our people, whoſe habits and whoſe honor it is to be induſtrious and ſelf-relying.

You may be aſked ſoon to join ſocieties that will decide your ſocial affinities through your college courſe. I am not well poſted up, indeed, as to the preſent condition of ſuch ſocieties, but I remember very well how matters ſtood at Cambridge in our day, and times have not probably wholly changed. There were ſome ſocieties which ſeemed to be baſed chiefly upon expenſive habits; and although their members denied this charge, and maintained that the aim was mainly to nurture gentlemanly taftes, and that the coft was not exceffive nor the conviviality extreme, it was evident, alike from the teftimony of feceders and the tendencies of the mafs of the actual members, that there was more pride and felf-indulgence than refinement or literature in the fpirit of the affociation. My own feeling is againft what were called the ariftocratic clubs in college; yet I had excellent friends who belonged to them, and who fuftained a high perfonal character. I cannot advife a young man, however ample his means, to join any affociation that tends to encourage the fpirit of focial or financial cafte, and flight distinctions of intellect and principle. I advife you not to join any club that muft feparate you from the majority of your clafs by its expenfe or ariftocratic exclufivenefs. The more fuch diftinctions are ignored in college the better, and the greater the opportunity for leaving the literary taftes and focial affections of ftudents to affociate in freedom. The only effential principles to be confidered in joining or eftablifhing college focieties are thofe that act upon character and attainments. That is the beft fociety that beft favors good fellowfhip and good fcholarfhip, and which is therefore moft open to the good fellows and good ſcholars, and to all who wiſh to become ſuch. It is well that there ſhould be an element of conviviality, but this ſhould be ſecondary, and within the limits of entire ſobriety; and even this conviviality will be more genuine if perſonal improvement is the main end, and the play is merrier becauſe it comes after the work that is to be done. I remember with great pleaſure four or five college ſocieties that were full of ſocial life and mental ſtimulus. The firſt of theſe was got up by a dozen or two of us in our Freſhman year, when we held debates in each other's rooms every fortnight, with no other revels than a cigar for thoſe who liked to ſmoke, and a parting ſupper at the end of the year, this latter being the only part of the hiſtory that does not win reſpect as I look back to it. This little club introduced ſome of us to the practice of extempore ſpeaking, which we have continued almoſt every week to the preſent time. Then came the "Inſtitute of 1770," a noble old ſociety, with regular debates and declamations, that were of great ſervice, alike in bringing out modeſt talent, and in forming a ſound college opinion. Then came the Haſty Pudding Club, with its fun as well as its philoſophy—its ſtories, ſongs, and bowls, and ſpoons, pudding, milk, butter, and molaſſes, as well as its eſſays and orations. If I remember rightly, I began my public life by giving the Haſty Pudding Oration, and remember with great pleaſure the ſocial and often brilliant evenings that we paſſed together over the huge iron pots, with their golden contents. The beſt of the college ſocieties, however, for intellectual improvement, was one that we formed in our day under the name of Harvard Union, under whoſe auſpices we heard the beſt debates that I ever had the good fortune to attend. This aſſociation was quite comprehenſive in its plan, and was open to the members of the two, and perhaps the three elder claſſes. The moſt weighty ſubjects were diſcuſſed with earneſtneſs and dignity, by youths, many of whom are now known in the prominent places in literature and the profeſſions. I think highly of the tendency of ſuch movements under good management, and am quite ſure that they not only improved the ſpeakers, but inſtructed and quickened the hearers, doing much to elevate the ſtandard of opinion in the college at large. I hear nothing of the Harvard Union now, but I hope that its place is held by ſome ſimilar inſtitution.

We ſometimes had voluntary meetings in preſence of our profeſſors, and of theſe I remember with eſpecial pleaſure our evenings with Chaucer and Spenſer at Profeſſor Edward T. Channing's ſtudy. How his genial face ſhone in the light of the winter's fire, and threw new meaning upon the rare gems of thought and humor and imagination of thoſe kings of ancient ſong. Who of us does not bleſs him every day that we write an Engliſh ſentence for his pure taſte and admirable ſimplicity? I remember well alſo a little coterie who met to declaim choice pieces of proſe and verſe with the profeſſor of elocution, our enthuſiaſtic friend, Dr. Barber. Thoſe twelve or fourteen youths have had various deſtinies, but none of them has made more mark in the world than the handſome, brilliant, free-and-eaſy fellow who uſed to declaim Byron with downturned collar, that ſhowed a throat ſmooth and full as a girl's. He ſpoke and wrote well, but we never expected Motley to read Dutch and write the Hiſtory of Holland.

Other organizations there are for ſpecial purpoſes, eſpecially for favorite amuſements, ſuch as are well known. So far as it is expedient to have companions in recreation, as in ball-playing or rowing, one muſt do so; but the leſs cumbrous the organization the better, and the freer each one is left to the uſe of his time and the range of his ſtudies and taſtes the better for him. There are ſometimes caſes of regular combinations for unworthy purpoſes—either equivocal pleaſures, or pernicious ideas and uſages. Againſt fellowſhips in smoke, and liquor, and ribaldry, I need not warn you, and I hope that there is no need now of warning any ſtudent of Harvard in theſe days. I hope that the ſocial life that prevails now, anſwers, and more than anſwers, to what was beſt in our time, and not only favors ſound morals, but alſo a free and earneſt faith. Perhaps the moſt memorable aſſociation in our college courſe was one decidedly religious, that we joined in our Senior year, and which was regularly tranſmitted to us from the previous claſs, with a record-book, which the late Judge Hopkinson brought to me at the time. It numbered members of every creed, from the freeſt to the ſtricteſt, upon a true Broad Church platform, and required each one in turn to prepare an original eſſay, and offer a prayer, either original or ſelected. I remember well when your father, then a youth in his teens, took his turn, and beſides reading an eſſay of his own, offered a free and fervent prayer that impreſſed all preſent, even thoſe of the ſtricteſt sects. Much fruit grew from this aſſociation, and it did much to decide the profeſſional career of ſome of the members. It will be well to continue ſuch an organization, although it is beſt not to have it ſo ſecret as was our cuſtom, and a proper degree of privacy may exiſt without ſecrecy. As an expreſſion of faith, however, nothing is ſo good as a direct connection with the Church, and I regret that ſo many of our earneſt young men left this ſtep till the cloſe of the college courſe. The more affectionate and cheerful ideas of religion that now prevail, make it eaſier for a genial and reverential ſtudent to become a communicant now than in the older times.

Some ſocieties that are now defunct, perhaps on account of being miſmanaged, ſeemed uſeful in our day as ſafety-valves of buoyant animal ſpirits; and I cannot but regret the demiſe of the Med. Fac., with its maſquerade and diablerie, which served as the true college carnival, and the Harvard Waſhington Corps, with its healthy drill, and valuable tribute to muſcle and energy. Other means, of courſe, will anſwer the ſame ends; but for my own part, I would rather ſee old cuſtoms reformed than abolifhed. The Med. Fac. frolic tempted to no inebriation, and was more innocent than a raid upon henroofts, or a covert vifit to the city; and the military corps gave more general activity, and developed better energy than is apt to come from the boat-clubs. But every generation muft fettle its own problems, and I am only saying that we had our way of fettling ours.

As to college focieties in general, I would advife you to be quite at eafe as to their fmiles or frowns, very fure that you will need none of them but fuch as help forward your culture; and your affinity for thefe will not fail to open them to you. As to purely convivial focieties, they will be likely to take time that you can pafs more profitably and pleafantly in your own way; but if you are afked to join occafionally in college pleafantries, you will be at little lofs to decide upon each cafe according to the parties and principles concerned. It is evident, however, that an earneft young man's focial nature cannot be fhut up within any fet organizations, and that he will move freely according to his affinities in the clafs and claffes at large. Moving thus freely he will ftill find that all habits and difpofitions tend to a more or lefs open organization, and that every clafs becomes virtually a fociety, animated by a few leading men and principles. It will have, on every fubject of conduct or opinion, its right, and left, and centre; and the pofition held by each member on a leading fubject is apt to decide his pofition on other fubjects. Thus induftry leads the right wing in the direction of faithful ftudy, and idlenefs gathers its truants on the left, and tries to maintain and vindicate its pofition by fome fhow of manlinefs or felf-fufficiency, and fometimes not wholly in mockery, diftributes its honors to its model dunces.

Morals and religion fhow fomething of the fame tendency as induftry, in developing their oppofites, and fometimes they identify their pofition with that of good fcholarship, and every found, confervative principle. The nature of fociety, whether in fchools or nations, thus will fhow itfelf, and youths, like men, will combine according to their dominant dispofitions, for men need fympathy to help them in well-doing or in ill-doing. I urge you to refpect duly the fympathetic element in education, and to win and give as much as you can of its bleffing. I urge you efpecially to underftand the force of a pofitive and aggreffive attitude in every good movement, and to ſeek ſuch companions as are not ſhaking in their ſhoes, but going bravely forward towards worthy ends—moſt earneſt yourſelf to enter into their ſpirit by joining them in their career. The trouble too often is with well-diſpoſed ſtudents, that they are timid and apologetic towards idlers and profligates, and ſometimes almoſt beg their pardon, inſtead of rebuking their folly, and ſtopping their inſults. The true poſition for rectitude is active and aggreſſive. *Momentum* is more than a match for *inertia,* and a little ball in motion knocks down eaſily ten great pins that are ſtationary. Let the good fellows and the good principles in college be in the active voice, true to their own inſtincts and true to each other, and before the four years' end, it will be found that the greateſt power goes with the beſt purpoſes, and not only have the good fellows kept their own ground, but that they have carried the war into the enemy's country, and won over to their ſide half the idlers and ſcoffers in the claſs. Remember this fact early; and where the true flag of honor, purity, and faith floats, there do not be aſhamed to ſhow yourſelf without fear and without preſumption.

I hope to ſpeak further of ſociety, more in its relations to the world outſide the college-walls.

IV.

THE STUDENT AND THE WORLD.

I TAKE a ſomewhat broader range, my dear friend, in theſe letters, than I at firſt intended, becauſe the circle of readers widens, and being aſked to write for other young men ſituated as you are, I prefer printing to copying out this ſeries of plain counſels. The ſubject now before us is the Student and the World, eſpecially the world of pleaſure and ſociality outſide the college walls.

There is ſomething half monkiſh and half military in the poſition of our collegians. The old univerſities were actually under monaſtic superviſion, and their cloiſters were not wholly unlike thoſe of the great monaſteries. Each college was a religious houſe that generally bore in its very name the ghoſtly preſtige of its origin. Our modern universities, such as the great ſeminaries of Germany, have the ſecluſion of the camp rather than of the convent, and are kept from the broad world more by exacting ſtudies, clanniſh temper, and rough manners, than by any excluſive rule. We ſee both ſpecimens of the ſtudent among ourſelves; and ſome pale recluſe who looks as if he had ſtepped out of the cloiſter, and never played with merry children, finds himſelf ſtartled at his midnight-lamp by the din from the room of his next neighbor, who is renowning it with a knot of like bloods over the brimming punch-bowl, in an atmoſphere of ſmoke as thick as that of the battle-field. Perhaps the military element generally predominates, and our ſtudents keep out of ſociety becauſe they prefer the rough ways of the college to the ſmooth ways of the drawing-room. The conſequence is, that like ſoldiers and ſailors, they ſuffer from the abſence of refining ſociety, eſpecially female ſociety, and inſtead of being ſaved from ſenſualiſm by the ſecluſion, they tend too much towards the groſs paſſions of the camp and the fleet.

On this account ſome reformers are for abandoning the collegiate life altogether, giving up the plan of rooming within the academic walls, and ſcattering the ſtudents throughout the homes of the city. But ſaying nothing of the expoſure of ſuch ſtudents as come from a diſtance, with no good home in the city, or near enough the college, it is clear that an advantage is loſt by ſeparating the young men from each other, and from the ſelf-relying diſcipline that life within the college halls ought to give. I am aware that the queſtion between the two ſyſtems is full of difficulties, but ſo far as I can judge from obſervation, I am compelled to give the preference to the old ſyſtem, and to regard thoſe inſtitutions as leaſt succeſsful that call their ſtudents together only for recitation, and then diſmiſs them to the excitements and pleaſures, or perhaps to the unwholeſome ſecluſion of home. It is not well, indeed, to allow the youth to forget home, and its delights and affections. Yet twelve weeks of vacation give ample opportunity to keep home feelings freſh, and the months of abſence, inſtead of chilling, ought to quicken the love for the old fireſide, which is never more precious than when ſeen in the enchantment of diſtance, and with the hope of return. The important point is to maintain a true ſtudent's ſecluſion without loſs of refinement and affection. This point may be reached without any departure from ſtudious habits or from ſocial intercourſe. A young man at college may not only find good ſociety among his claſſmates, but he has ample opportunity for quiet and profitable ſociality among families near by. If at Cambridge, he may uſe his leiſure Saturday to the great advantage of his health and ſpirits by viſiting friends in town, or in the neighboring towns, or by ſeeing the arts, and perhaps hearing the muſic of the city. If he employs his Saturdays and his vacations well, he can be a faithful ſtudent without becoming an anchorite or a clown.

A queſtion often comes up as to the propriety of a collegian's frequenting evening parties, or accepting ſuch invitations as frequently come to him, eſpecially if he has many relatives and friends in the neighborhood. A little candid thought will meet the queſtion at once, and diſtinguiſh between the occaſional ſocial viſiting that refreſhes and encourages a youth, and the round of diſſipation that fevers and weakens him. It is beſt for a ſtudent at Cambridge to keep wholly out of the round of faſhionable dinners and parties. They are wholly incompatible with fidelity to his ſtudies. To go to Boſton and ſit three or four hours at a great dinner, is worſe for him than two days' leſſons in one; and to endure the heat, and air, and eating and drinking of an evening party or ball, of the uſual pattern, is worſe than a week's midnight ſtudy with quiet and temperance. Beſides, ſuch viſits are immenſely prodigal of time; and a youth who viſits much in the great world is a ſpendthrift of his hours and his thoughts at once. He is alſo in great danger of becoming a poor trifler, and making amuſement the occupation inſtead of the incident of his life. He is tempted, alſo, to form engroſſing and fooliſh intimacies; and if he eſcapes the inglorious fate of being the Æolian attachment to ſome flighty girl's piano, or the poodle in her leading-ſtrings, he may fall into the equally hurtful ſnare of general coquetry, and become one of thoſe habitual admirers of the sex, thoſe profeſſed lady's men, whom men diſlike and true women abominate.

Without any ſuch extreme, without being a diner-out or a party-goer, a ſtudious youth may eaſily keep up his ſocial intereſts, and live within the refining and idealizing influence of good female ſociety. He has one day of the week expreſſly at his command, and he may add to the cuſtomary Saturday an occaſional Sunday for viſiting friends, if his own home is too far diſtant. He will not fail to make pleaſant acquaintances in the families of his claſſmates, which will make his leiſure days agreeable; and within the ſhadow of the univerſity itſelf he will find homes open to him which he may viſit with pleaſure and profit. The kind of ſociality that prevails in a univerſity town is generally of a quiet and wholeſome kind, and a ſtudent who chats or dances an hour or two in good company, and is back in his room an hour before midnight, may once a week or fortnight repeat the experiment without harm to health or philoſophy. It is an excellent thing to combine healthful exerciſe with ſociality, as when alone or with a friend or two you walk a few miles into the country, and calling on ſome acquaintance for an hour, you return with clearer brain and lighter heart, to welcome ſtudies and to a ſounder ſleep.

College life, although given to ſtudies called by eminence liberal, has its own forms of narrowneſs; and ſtudents are often full of poor prejudices. Their frequent error is to underrate the buſineſs and the men of the world, and to meaſure intellectual power purely by a bookiſh ſtandard. It is well for them, therefore, to mingle with the leaders of the actual world, and learn for themſelves the ſuperior ſtrength and point of a practical over a merely ſcholaſtic training. I adviſe you to call on bufinefs men fometimes at their ftores and factories, to look upon the wharves and fhip-yards, to hear once in a while a good argument in court, and to affure yourfelf that all knowledge and power are not fhut up within the walls of the univerfity. It is good, alfo, to keep up a clofe acquaintance with the foil and its tillers, and you muft not lofe your frequent opportunities of vifiting the country places that offer you a free range over the fields, as well as a welcome feat at the table. For want of fuch contact with the great world, and its work, many ftudents become hopelefly fcholaftic, and the pale caft that ficklies over their face is not fo much the ftamp of the prefence of thought, as of the abfence of active force and practical aim. Mind and body will be gainers by a more pofitive tone, and the ftyle of compofition and manners muft win energy in this practical fchool. The peculiar intellectual failing of fedentary men—a dreamy, *fubjective* turn of thought and fancy—will be checked; and in writing, fpeaking, and fcheming, a healthy, effective, *objective* manner will be encouraged. Too many ftudents write and fpeak as one that beateth the air. Contact with practical men will move them to give up their rhetorical flourifhes, and hit the nail on the head. The great claffic writers, Homer and Demofthenes at the top of them, have a remarkably direct and bufinefs ftyle of utterance; and they who would underftand and win anything of their power muft learn to look, as they did, to the great world of facts and deeds.

As the ftudent's fubjectivity may be profitably corrected by contact with the world's reality, fo his too cold and heavy and formal intellectualism may be corrected by affociation with the vivacity and grace and infight of refined and gifted women. As humanity is both mafculine and feminine, the true human culture fhould be fo too, and no young man can be well educated by men alone. Without arguing the queftion of opening colleges to both fexes, I am convinced that our ftudents owe fome of the worft defects of their ftyle and thinking to exclufively mafculine teachers and companions, and if they would converfe more with bright women, they would be faved from much of that dull fcholaftic profing which is the incubus on college diction, and they would win a colloquial eafe which is the fineft grace of ftyle, and the effential of effective eloquence. It will be well for you to vifit in families where converfation is interefting and quickening; and if two or three houfeholds are open to you where fenfible mothers and fprightly daughters combine their gifts, you may find yourfelf as much profited as pleafed by the fociality.

An advantage more important than that which is merely intellectual comes from good female fociety. True women feel more than moft men the higher realities of life, and are able without any labored preaching or moralizing to imprefs a young man with a living fenfe of divine things. There is an ideality in their nature greater than they often comprehend in their thinking; or, in other words, they are often wifer and better than they know, and can *infpire* more than they can *teach.* Nothing gives a youth a more vital and effective ideal of life, than the beft female fociety, and more corrects the fenfualifm that grows out of natural inftincts unchecked. EMERSON wifely remarks that the fexual paffion feems to be immenfely overloaded, and its power is probably proof of the determination of nature to keep and continue her own. He might go on to illuftrate the remarkable correctives of this paffion through the higher affections and ideas that true feminine fociety infpires. Duly cultivated, those very inftincts that ruin fo many by debafing exceffes yield exalting motives, as the rank earth, which worms may infeſt and weeds may cover, will, under true culture, produce fair lilies and ſweet roſes. The ideal ſenſe which ſenſible and refined women nurture in young men marvelloufly helps their morals as well as their intellect, and when united with loyal habits of ſtudy and judicious methods of exerciſe, keeps down the groſſer paſſions, and does much to keep the ſenſes where they had better reſt until manhood awakens them into full conſciousneſs, and God's law does not refuſe its ſanction.

I hope to write a letter or two more of this ſeries, and treat of perſonal habits and religious principles.

V.

PERSONAL HABITS.

It has ſeemed to me, eſpecially of late years, as I have obſerved more the ways of men, and tried to ſtudy better the nature of human power, that the philoſophy of habit is very inadequately underſtood, and that we are too apt to aſcribe to a merely mechanical routine the reſults that come from the recurrent play of vital forces. Three moments of chief importance are to be noted in the order of our habits: Firſt, we note the beginning, which generally joins an idea to an action, as when a child begins to eat bread, and aſſociates the ſight or idea of bread with the act of taking and maſticating it. According to this view, a habit begins in the union of *ſenſe* with *activity*. Secondly, we note the recurrence, which either by an external or internal cauſe repeats the union, and the idea of the thing ſought renews the ſeeking of it, as when the child who has taſted bread is led to ſeek it again, ſo as to form a more or lefs regular cuftom of eating. Thirdly, we note the bearing of the feveral claffes of habits upon each other, as when the child is trained to adjuft the hours of eating to the hours of fleep, exercife, ftudy, or play. We gain great light upon our own felf-difcipline, if we ftudy our ways in this manner, and afk ourfelves what practices we have begun, how often they tend to recur, and how they harmonize with one another, efpecially how effectually the higher tendencies mafter the lower, and the nobleft habits regulate the more fenfual and material.

Viewed in this light, what immenfe importance attaches to the years of ftudent life, when a youth, no longer under the fchoolmafter's eye, is left so much to himfelf, and away from the watch of home and family, is to form thofe methods of thought and action that are very likely to go with him through life! It is evident that the higheft felf-control or the loweft felf-indulgence may be made the dominant cuftom, and thus become a fecond nature. It is never, indeed, too late for a man to repent; but furely he who carries from college into the world habits of indolence and diffipation, however bitterly he repents of his folly, muft bear fome of its fruits with him to his dying day. In youth, as we learn languages ſo eaſily, we alſo learn that higher art of articulation—the pronouncing of our ſenſes and powers into diſtinct and expreſſive habits. Not only do the feet beſt learn to dance in youth, but the whole of our nature beſt learns to walk its choral round, and mind and heart and will may keep ſtep with the hours to the cheering muſic that is made by the pulſe-beats of young and healthy blood.

A true ſyſtem of habits has its foundation in the ordering of oui bodily inſtincts and appetites, eſpecially in duly adjuſting or balancing the receptive and active functions. He is a healthy man who adjuſts properly the thought and action that exhauſt his ſtrength with the food and ſleep that reſtore it, and who in like manner keeps up the balance between his ſenſitive nerves and active muſcles by relieving excitement of nerves by active exerciſe, and quickening muſcular ſolidity by nervous ſenſibility. The law of polarity, which pervades all creation, is eminently powerful in the human conſtitution; and all true life, whether of body or mind, comes from the harmony of forces that ſeem to be antagoniſts.

The moſt obvious polar diverſity is that which contraſts our ſleeping with our waking hours, and almoſt repeats the images of death and life. How long we ought to ſleep I do not undertake to ſay with poſitive certainty, ſo widely do different perſons vary, and ſo much do many people err from the truth by counting as ſleep only their hours of being in bed, whilſt they never ſeem to be fully awake even at noon-day, and others who lounge half the time in bed are rarely ſound aſleep. If I were to try to ſtate the true rule for ſleep, according to the beſt experience and obſervation, it would be eight hours, and ſurely never leſs than ſeven. A ſtudent needs, probably, more ſleep than a laboring man, alike becauſe his brain is more uſed (and the brain ſuffers more than the muſcles from overaction), and becauſe, moreover, the ſtudent is ſo apt to carry the thoughtfulneſs of ſtudy to his pillow as to find it hard to drop into ſlumber at once, as the tired workman generally does. I adviſe you to be very careful to ſecure regular and ſufficient ſleep; and in moſt caſes when you are tempted by peculiar anxiety to ſit up very late, and win ſtudy at the coſt of an excited brain, it is better to think more of keeping the inſtrument ſound than of forcing the work. I have ſuffered ſometimes by continual late ſtudy, and have kept at my pen till morning. Now, I prefer a healthy brain to an elaborate manuſcript, and am ſurer of ſucceſs in ſuch emergencies by ſpeaking extempore from a clear and cool head, than by reading a diſcourſe that has been written by the midnight lamp. I do not believe in the midnight lamp at all, and adviſe you to be on your pillow always at leaſt an hour before that witching time. In ſummer it is well for a ſtudent to go to bed at ten and riſe at six, or half an hour before, and in winter he may retire and riſe an hour later. As to any conſiderable ſtudy before breakfaſt, I do not recommend it, and am inclined to think as poorly of morning candle-light as of the midnight lamp. I tried once to ſteal time for tranſlating a work from the German by early morning ſtudy, and the ſymptoms of a nervous fever that appeared in the courſe of a few weeks led me never to repeat the experiment.

As to hours of ſtudy, they ſhould never exceed thoſe now made the limit of manual labor—ten hours—and I believe that ſix hours of cloſe application will in the long run accompliſh more good work than twelve hours. If a youth actually ſtudies ſix hours, and adds to this the time ſpent in going to and from recitation, and in waiting for others to recite, he will find very little of the working part of the day left. If we add to ſix hours of actual work over books the time uſually given by an earneſt ſtudent to thought, and reading, and inſtructive converſation, it will be found that twelve out of the twenty-four hours are generally given to the culture of the mind. Stating my views in another way, I can ſay that there is wiſdom in dividing the day into three parts of eight hours each—one part for ſleep; one for ſuch exertion of the mind as may be called ſtudy, whether learning leſſons or taſking the thoughts by ſolid reading or careful meditation; one part for recreation, or for all that refreſhes ſoul and body by food, exerciſe, ſociety, and all ſuch intellectual occupations as belong more to the play rather than to the work of the mind. I do not, of courſe, mean to ſay that theſe three parts ſhould be ſeparated by a rigid line, and that recreation and ſtudy ſhould occupy each eight conſecutive hours. It is beſt for one not to give more than two conſecutive hours to one object; and he is wiſe who goes from one ſtudy to another, or interſperſes ſtudy with exerciſe or converſation, ſo as to ſecure conſtant freſhneſs and life. The Jeſuits, who are marvellouſly ſhrewd in their way, forbid their pupils from ſtudying more than two hours without intermiſſion; and Voltaire, who ſo hated the Jeſuits, copied their ſagacity by keeping ſometimes four deſks in his library, with an unfiniſhed work on each, and going, as he was moved, from one to the other, as poetry, hiſtory, criticiſm, or philoſophy invited him. You will do well to ſtudy a judicious alternation in the diviſion of your time and ſtudies, being eſpecially careful to ſweeten hard and repulſive branches by ſuch as are more pleaſant, and in every way to change the poſture of your mind, ſo as to refreſh and relieve the more weary faculties. Thus you will really ſtudy, and not pretend to do ſo, as is the way with many who pore liſtleſſly over the book hour after hour, and are about as much wiſer at the end as the ſpaniel at their feet, or the bird in the window.

As to the things of the table—in our day we were not tempted as you may be. We boarded in commons, and paid, I think, but a dollar and ninety cents a week for board—a ſum that did not furniſh many alluring luxuries. The ſimplicity of this fare ſometimes tempted us to make up for it by ſome little refection in our rooms, and not a few carried this practice to an injurious extent by exceffive eating and drinking in the evening. It is beft for a ftudent to live amply, but plainly, and be content with what is fet upon a good family-table. I confider all that is eaten after the regular meals as worfe than ufelefs; and many of our ftout fellows owed the caufe of their dyfpepfia and "blues" to the frequent punch and mince-pies that made their evening entertainment. As to wine and ardent fpirits, the lefs of them fo much the better; and without reviving the Mohammedan doctrine that makes it a fin in itfelf to tafte the juice of the grape, it is enough to fay that the young fellow who has not enough of the wine of life in his heart to keep him merry and up to any genial fport, without stimulants, is a difgrace to youthful humanity. Moft ftudents who ufe wine repent of it moft bitterly, and I never knew one who abftained from it to regret the felf-denial. Without taking any afcetic ground, or being wifer than the Gofpel, I advife you to keep wholly out of college caroufals, and to have no incentives to fuch indulgence in your room. I fay the fame of tobacco; and whilft your companions will do as they choofe, I hope that you will let this potent weed alone, and will be free from its ſmell and its poiſon. They who uſe it never adviſe others to begin the practice. I can speak from the oppoſite experience; and never having uſed it in any form, attribute ſomewhat of my uniform health, in ſpite of a delicate conſtitution, to my abſtinence. I think the habit unclean and pernicious, inviting frequent potations by artificial thirſt, and ſtimulating the nervous ſyſtem, and depraving the whole ſenſitive organiſm.

In judging of the harm done by the leading vices to which youth is tempted, it is well to judge of them by three teſts—*quantity*, *quality*, and *relation*—according to the categories of the new logic. Some vices are ſuch merely from quantity, or overſtepping a certain limit, as gluttony, which is wrong, not becauſe it is eating, but becauſe it is exceſſive eating. Other vices are ſuch from their eſſential quality, ſuch as licentiouſneſs, which is wrong in its firſt ſtep, and in its beginning it ſhould be wholly checked. The proper as well as the eaſieſt rule for governing the inſtincts that lead to licentiouſneſs is to keep them in check, and preöccupy the mind with wholeſome thoughts and affections, and regulate the body by juſt diet and activity. It is eaſier to be wholly correct than partly so; and as to all vices of sensualism, I can do no better than quote the emphatic remark of Professor ERDMANN, of Halle, in his recent lectures on Academic Life and Study. Distinguishing between conviviality and licentiousness, he maintains that he who intrudes precociously into the temple of Bacchus dishonors the temple, but commits no sacrilege. "He is guilty of sacrilege, however, who, without being initiated by the consecration of nature, thievishly skulks into the mysteries of Aphrodite, and of double the sin if he makes a beast of himself in this forbidden temple." It is idle to try to maintain that purity of life costs no struggle in youth, but it is worse than idle to deny that the victory may be secured, and the whole culture is deepened and exalted by the conquest.

As to vices of relation, the best example may be taken from the use of money. The waste of money is in all cases wrong, but even the spending of it for things unobjectionable in themselves, but not essential to living, is very wrong when it is beyond a student's just means, and becomes oppressive to parents in limited circumstances. What can be meaner than for a student to indulge himself in expenſes for dreſs and amuſements and coſtly books, and matters of taſte, whilſt his parents are ſtruggling to pay his term-bills, and even the frugal houſehold is more scanty becauſe of the effort to give him an education? The wrong becomes monſtrous when diſſipation, as is ſometimes the caſe, attends prodigality, and the ſon allows his family at home to pinch their table and wardrobe, whilſt he feaſts and rides like an heir of fortune, and is perhaps ſent home in diſgrace and debt, the mortification as well as the ruin of his father. Let not the rich man's ſon think himſelf exempt from this outrage, if he ſquanders the time and opportunity that are more than gold, and returns his father's toil and mother's love by indolence or vice, and mortifies the whole family by his nothingneſs or perverſity, waſting a life that is more precious than money.

As to bodily exerciſe, ſo much is ſaid of its importance now, that I need not treat it at length. You muſt never forget that muſcular activity is the natural offset to nervous excitement, and take ſuch exerciſe as your opportunities and conſtitution dictate. You do not wiſh, however, to become a pugiliſt or ſtevedore; and it is important to prefer the exercifes that brace the nerves and infpirit the mind, to thofe that merely fwell the mufcles, and tend to vulgarize the form and movements. For this aim the knightly arts and fports are better than the common gymnaftics.

One letter on morals and religion will clofe this feries.

VI.

MORALS AND RELIGION.

THE letters of this ſeries, thus far, my dear friend, have all, indeed, treated directly or indirectly of morals and religion, and perhaps have ſaid or implied enough to ſhow the foundations upon which a ſtudent's life ſhould be built. Yet a few points may properly be preſented with ſome urgency, as touching the moſt prominent temptations of his poſition, and probable defects of his character. Of courſe, there can be but one eſſential morality and religion, yet the principles that in themſelves are as univerſal as truth itſelf, have eſpecial applications to peculiar conditions and claſſes.

Morality we regard as true life in its human relations, whilſt religion is life in its relations with God. The two are cloſely connected with each other, but are not identical; and whilſt morality ought to be under God, or animated by a religious ſpirit, its own ſphere is human, and it may, indeed, in its largeſt ſenſe, be called true humanity. Taking the ſimpleſt of all diviſions, we regard morality as in its eſſence the love of man, and as having two main branches —honor and juſtice—the one being the true love of ſelf, and the other the true love of our neighbor. In both branches of moral duty, honor and juſtice, the ſtudent is likely to be very defective.

What is more common than falſe honor or ſpurious ſelf-reſpect in college life? True ſelf-reſpect centres upon what is worthieſt in perſonal character, and finds ſatisfaction in purity, wiſdom, fidelity, reverence, and in all thoſe qualities that ſubdue the paſſions and impulſes to reaſon and conſcience. College honor is very apt to ſet up the paſſions and impulſes as maſters, and make manlineſs conſiſt in ſelf-will. This ſelf-will is ſometimes ſenſual, and then it affects to put the cap of ſacred liberty upon the harlot head of ſenſualiſm, and you have already ſeen, probably, ſome of the worſt vices defended by the ſtolen name of independence. Or wilfulneſs may take a higher form, and may claim to make a law of itſelf or of its own coterie, in defiance of human and divine law. We ought to be ready, indeed, to excuſe ſome little reſtiveneſs on the part of the faculty of will, ſome little range of antics and running and prancing before the fiery ſteed is ſubdued to the maſter's hand. But let us beware of calling the faults of rude nature virtues, and defending them as fortreſſes, inſtead of paſſing them as ſtepping-ſtones. The youth who baſes his own dignity upon the amount of his defiance towards his ſuperiors, may be very ſure that he meaſures himſelf by as perverſe a rule as he who would meaſure his property by the amount of his frauds, and ſo confound his arrears with his aſſets. Nor does a youth enhance his own dignity by joining a little coterie of free companions, and making war with them upon public opinion, ſober judgment, and careful induſtry. In ſome way, moſt collegians are tempted to fall into ſome form of this falſe honor, and to join in ſome kind of rebellion againſt principles or inſtitutions which in maturer years they learn to reſpect. Self-will is always ſure to ſet up its prerogative as central, inſtead of centring itſelf upon the eternal right; and whilſt in aſtronomy you will find the Copernican ſyſtem reigning without a rival, you will not fail to diſcover that many bright wits rule their lives upon the Ptolemaic theory, and act as if their own dark and earthy will were the centre of the moral univerſe.

The obvious tendency of ſuch falſe honor is towards injuſtice, and he who does not truly reſpect himſelf cannot readily reſpect his neighbor. He who eſtimates his own conſequence by his amount of ſelf-will, of courſe looks down upon all perſons whom he can browbeat, and tries to feed his own conceit by throwing contempt upon others, pampering pride and vanity perhaps at once, by inſulting thoſe whom he ought to reſpect, that he may win plaudits from thoſe whom he ought to rebuke, if not to deſpiſe. The injuſtice that is the offspring of falſe honor ſhows itſelf in college in various ways, ſometimes in annoying fellow-ſtudents, ſometimes in aſſaulting or plundering the townſpeople, and ſometimes by conſpiring againſt the college government. Sometimes, indeed, a certain paſſion for fun is more prominent than any depraved ſpirit of miſchief; yet ſuch fun, when perſiſtently purſued, ends in habitual miſchief, and has left a mark upon many a youth's fortune and diſpoſition that years cannot obliterate. In every claſs there is more or leſs diſpoſition to oppreſs the more ſenſitive of its own members, whilſt there is a ſtanding cuſtom of annoying to the utmoſt all novices in the lower claſſes. I have no objection to giving the greenhorns a little good-natured initiation, but when it comes to perſonal inſults, injury to property, falſehood, and theft, the joke goes too far; and I have known outrages to be committed by ſtudents upon their fellows, eſpecially of the younger claſſes, that no ſophiſtry could call by any other name than ruffianly and daſtardly, as mean as they were inſolent, becauſe ſo ſure of doing harm with impunity. You may already find that the idlers of the claſs conſpire againſt the induſtrious, and that ſome of the beſt fellows in the claſs are ridiculed as "digs." Never mind it, if your turn comes, and you find yourſelf for a ſeaſon in this proſcribed ſet. The tables will ſoon be turned, and the very ſcapegraces who once worried you will be coming to you to help them with their leſſons, to write their themes for them, and perhaps to encourage them to make decent men of themſelves. In four years the meaning of the term *dig* changes, and from being a term of menial reproof, it becomes the firſt ſyllable of *dig*nity.

As to wrongs to perſons outſide the college walls, ſuch as are done in ſtreet-fights, robbery of orchards and hen-rooſts, it is important to remember that the Homeric age has paſſed away, that piracy is no longer heroifm, and to knock down a policeman or to plunder farms is felony. The fooner ftudents underftand that they are bound by the law of the land, the better for their morals and their mirth, and the fooner they will be moved to let their neighbor's goods alone, and to feek fport in more free and congenial fields.

In refpect to the college government, the too common feeling among ftudents is one of antagonifm, and I furely do not think that all the blame in this matter is on one fide. I do not think that profeffors and tutors generally fhow enough perfonal intereft and regard for their pupils to win from them the true favor. The two parties are too often found fet againft each other in mutual fufpicion, each miftrufting and miftrufted. The firft ftep to a better underftanding might be wifely taken by the inftructors, and more perfonal kindnefs on their part will be fure to win new confidence from the better clafs of ftudents. But no amount of referve on the part of profeffors and tutors can juftify the wanton affaults upon college order that are fo often dignified by the name of rebellion. If a ftudent regards himfelf as unjuftly dealt with, he can ftate his grievance, and be fure of a hearing. If the ſtatement does not win favor, and remove the grievance, he can voluntarily leave college in a ſpirit that will be ſure to win reſpect from friends, and not cloſe other inſtitutions againſt him. The reſort to uproar and inſult, aſſaults on college property, and indignity towards perſons, is invariably as unhappy in reſult as falſe in principle. College rebellions coſt the rebels very dear, and are always a loſing operation to the authors. One of the worſt aſpects in which they preſent themſelves to a graduate in after years, is their diſhonor towards inſtitutions that ought to be held ſacred. The youth who diſgraces his parents diſgraces himſelf; and thoſe ſtudents who try to throw a ſtain upon their Alma Mater muſt ere long ſee that, could they ſucceed, they would ſhame themſelves. It is well that all college rebellions in our quarter have left our good mother's name unſullied. Sometimes, indeed, great wrong is done to individual officers, and the inſtructors who are more offenſive from ſome infelicity of manner or temper than from any incapacity or ſelfiſhneſs, are made the butt of general wrath. It may repreſs many a hot-headed youth's ferocity againſt an unpopular tutor, to be told that ſometimes a feeble conſtitution is miſtaken for a sullen temper, and that a hard ſtruggle with poverty and ill-health may give an expreſſion that looks like ſeverity. Sometimes even diffidence is taken for conceit, and the teacher who hardly preſumes to claim affection in his humility is treated as an iceberg of indifference, if not of pride. Of college officers in general, it may be ſaid that, conſidering their gifts and culture, they have ſcanty returns of emolument, and it is great injuſtice to add to their limitation by unkindneſs or diſreſpect. The ſtudent who has the true ſenſe of honor in himſelf, will have true juſtice towards others; and among the reforms that we long to ſee carried out in our colleges is the inauguration of a purer moral ſenſe in its twin virtues of juſtice and honor. A dozen noble ſpirits in any claſs may make a new era in their own career, and a dozen claſſes thus guided would bring in a new age in college ethics.

Such reſults cannot, however, come without motive from ſuperhuman ſources, and to religion we muſt look for the effective inſpiration. When morality becomes active, and not being content with ſhunning faults, it ſeeks poſitive virtues, it muſt follow an authority above itſelf. In fact, the true humanity is of neceſſity religious, and whilſt it ſeeks to be true to man, it can be ſo only in the filial ſpirit that treats him as God's creature and image. The youth who thus derives his morality from religion has a deeper ſenſe of human worth in himſelf and others, and his honor and juſtice riſe into a religious rectitude. He is moved not only to keep himſelf from harm, but to bring himſelf into fellowſhip with all goodneſs as the true honor. He is called not only to avoid injury to others, but to encourage in them every worthy hope, and ſo juſtice becomes poſitive righteouſneſs.

There is ſome difficulty in defining religion to the ſatisfaction of earneſt young people, and often they who are fond of the thing do not like the definition. It is very ſafe, however, to ſay that religion is our true relation towards God, and the fruit of it is a filial conſcience, true to him in a ſenſe of dependence and a ſenſe of duty. Harm is done when either of theſe elements is neglected, as when a ſhallow rationaliſm ſubſtitutes a mere doctrine as to God, or a mere opinion about him, for a living and perſonal truſt in him, or when a dry moraliſm puts a code of rules, a dead legaliſm, in place of the loving ſervice of the living God. The eſpecial bleſſing of the Goſpel is, that it reveals him in Chriſt as the ground of faith and obedience, and adds to the light of the incarnate Word the life of the animating Spirit. It is a bleſſed day for a ſtudent when he takes the Goſpel home to his own ſtudy and life. Study is radiant when it ſeeks for truth under the Eternal Light, and life is rich and vigorous when the purpoſes are cheered by the Eternal Spirit. I need not urge you to ſhun all perſonal aſſumption, and every trace of cant; but all the more earneſtly I exhort you to put yourſelf on the true ground, and make your education a gift of God's grace, as well as a work of your own labor, and your teacher's care.

I do not adviſe you to talk a great deal in a conſpicuous way on religious ſubjects, or to make any frequent profeſſions of faith. Let what you do ſay be very decided, and let your action be poſitive. Nothing is more decided than an habitual place at the communion-table, and a tongue reverential and pure. In all matters in which your convictions may conflict with notions of college honor, or condemn what eaſy conſciences and enticing pleaſures ſanction, you will be wiſe to take your own courſe early and ſtrongly, and let your actions ſpeak louder than words. In this way you will be true, and alſo influential, and you will ſtand forth as a manly Chriſtian, without loſing your name as a good fellow. You are not in danger of running into any morbid pietiſm, and I therefore need not warn you againſt the danger of ſtraining to become a ſaint in ſuch a way as to ceaſe to be a wholeſome, hearty man. Be a true man and a true Chriſtian, and your college life will be a world of riches to you that years will ever more develop. When you are as old as your father and I are, you will find the old times at Cambridge coming back with an ever-increaſing power; and when the charm of memory carries with it the light and peace of God's Word and Spirit and Church, college life is a fountain which pours its bleſſed waters on the path with ever freer flow, and refreſhes us in manhood with the ſparkling tide that ſo cheered us in our early days.

I little thought of writing ſo much when I ſent you that firſt ſtray letter; yet I have found ſatisfaction in the ſubject, and am quite ſure of having ſpoken with candor and earneſtneſs. God's bleſſing reſt upon you, and may your four years at college be to you and your parents all that your diſpoſitions promiſe, and their affection deſerves.

VII.

PROSPECTS AND RETROSPECTS.

My dear Friend—I will confeſs that I feel quite a new ſenſation at ſtanding upon ſuch terms of good will with the tenants of our old college rooms, and it gives me almoſt a new experience of youth to be aſſured that I have readers there who think that my off-hand counſels are worth publication. It is true, as you ſay, that the claſs of 1864 muſt be expected to differ in ſome reſpects from the claſs of 1832, and certainly the new generation ought to improve upon the old, although I need not tell you that difference is not of neceſſity improvement.

In ſome reſpects you have made decided improvements ſince our day, and I am ſure that there is more of genial and ideal aſſociation with claſs-fellowſhip than was uſual with us. There is ſtill room for progreſs, and college life would be marvelloußly transformed if every feſtival were as beautiful as the famous claſs day which is now kept, from year to year, in a way far beyond and above what we knew in our time. Why fhould not our ftudent life in America do fomething to give a better æfthetic and intellectual tone to American fociety? Why fhould not ftudents give us a true ideal of refinement and enthufiafm, of the true chivalry and the nobleft loyalty, as well as of dafhing courage and genial fellowfhip. I find myfelf thinking more and more of the reflex influence of clafs meetings and affociations. The human foul has a rhythm of its own that fets all its deeper experiences to mufic, and brings them ringing anew to our ears with each revolving year. Remember that you are not only ftocking your memory with commodities, but tuning it with melodies and harmonies, and for good or evil, the fcenes and companionfhips of thefe college-years are to fing themfelves to you again as long as you live. Try to live in fuch a way as to make the recollection of college life not only pleafant but elevating, and to induce you to continue the old friendfhips as part of your religion as well as your good-fellowfhip.

I advife you to keep carefully all important memorials of your college career, efpecially your text-books, compofitions, letters, notes of lectures, etc.

It is well alſo to keep a diary of thoughts, events, and friendſhips. This will help you in the maſtery of language, and be of great ſervice as a book of reference in after years. If you chooſe you might illuſtrate it with photographs of familiar faces that ſhall speak to you in time to come of ſcenes and friends long ago. Your text books will ſerve you not only as a remembrance to enjoy but an authority to conſult, for you can find the information you ſeek for eaſier in familiar manuals than in new and ſtrange volumes. Many a chance mark or ſtray pencilling on your Homer or Tacitus will call up the old times like a magic ſpell. Treaſure up too the devout books that you now read, and make them bleſs you evermore.

If you have health and proſperity you will in four years graduate, and count a new era from 1864. To ſet you thinking of your own future—and its bearings on your preſent—I ſend you a copy of the addreſs made to our claſs twenty-five years after graduating, and alſo of Rev. Charles J. Brook's beautiful poem. Your father ſat in the chair, and the ſpeaker was your friend and correſpondent. I likewiſe add a few miſcellaneous thoughts and recollections bearing upon ſtudent life, which I have reviſed from my papers as having ſome intereſt for you.

VIII.

HEART AND HEAD IN EDUCATION.

FROM AN ORATION BEFORE THE HASTY PUDDING CLUB IN UNIVERSITY HALL, FEBRUARY 22, 1831.

NUNQUAM aliud natura, aliud sapientia dicit—Wiſdom never denies the voice of nature. Such was the exclamation of Rome's laſt poet, Juvenal, in the decline of his country's glory. He ſaw the degeneracy of the age, the general licentiouſneſs, the many cauſes tending to turn the individual mind from its natural courſe, and he cried out againſt ſuch a perverſion of nature. We may join in this exclamation, ſaying in joy what he ſaid in ſorrow. In this age, in this country, and ſurely upon this birthnight of Waſhington, we may juſtly believe that natural rights are not to be trodden under foot, either in the ſtate or the academy. We ſhall not depart from the ſpirit of this occaſion by ſaying a few words now upon education as making men truer to nature.

The human mind is one whole, made up of various parts. To preſerve the ſeveral parts in their due proportion, to give each its own place and the exerciſe of its natural functions, ſhould be the object of education. This end cannot be attained if the mind is left wholly to itſelf, for in that caſe unpropitious circumſtances, as well as inordinate impulſes and fancies, may keep back ſome parts and bring others forward unduly. It is the office of poſitive culture to make or keep the balance of character. Much has been ſaid of the importance of keeping the intellectual powers in harmony with each other, but far too little notice has been taken of the connexion between the moral affections and the intellectual powers, or the influence of the heart upon the head. Let us conſider now the bearing of the moral upon the intellectual nature, that we may the better ſee what muſt be the prevailing motive force when the mind has its healthy natural tone.

I. Moral purity is needed in order to concentrate the powers and apply them to the deſired end. It is of courſe neceſſary to ſelf-control—to government of the thoughts. Now this ſelf-control beginning in the affections cannot end there, but may readily be transferred to the intellectual ſphere. From a command over the paſſions and over the thoughts ariſing from them, command is won over the thoughts in general and the ability to give them their juſt direction. This ability is needed by all minds, but eſpecially by thoſe who give themſelves to philoſophic meditation rather than to the chance impulſes of the hour. The philoſopher needs perfect equanimity, the utmoſt freedom from distracting impulſes and fancies. We find accordingly that they who have made the moſt diſtinguiſhed progreſs in ſcience, whether phyſical or metaphyſical, have been remarkable generally for moral purity, from the days of Archimedes and Plato to thoſe of Newton and Kant. Indeed it is next to impoſſible that a man abandoned to the movements of paſſion and the agitations of impulſe, ſhould poſſeſs the unwearied patience, the conſecutive thought, eſſential to the purſuit of ever-fleeing truth. There is, moreover, a cheerful ſerenity ſpringing from well-ordered affections, that contributes much to laſting ſatiſfaction and ſucceſs in literary purſuits. It is like the calm of a fair day, when the powers of nature are moſt effective becauſe moſt in harmony, and the elements and mankind are moſt buſily and happily at work.

II. Again, moral purity has a good influence over the particular turn of the taftes, and is a great fecurity againft many prejudices in this direction. When it is faid that a man has a tafte for any particular purfuit, the fact is not fo much that this tafte was an original gift as that it is the refult of the whole internal life. Now as the paffions and affections carry a confiderable vote in the mental cabinet, the turn taken by the whole mind muft depend much upon their difcipline. The paffions certainly have great influence over the opinions, making fome opinions more agreeable than others, and adding weight therefore to all the arguments in their behalf. Thus paffion is virtually a prejudice—a prejudice which all faithful moral difcipline tends to remove. In the words of the French philofopher, Degerando, "The advantages which the mathematical fciences owe to their very nature, virtue communicates to other branches of knowledge. For the mathematical fciences admit of cool and impartial inveftigation, becaufe they are not the fubjects of paffion."

III. Moral excellence infpires a love of method that delights in juft analyfis and arrangement. The order of exact moral difcipline leads the mind to a fimilar order in all that comes to its attention, and fuggefts the fyftem fo effential to clearnefs of thought and expreffion. Befides cordial and healthy affections delight in union, in intellectual as well as focial harmony. Now why fhould not this benevolence become an intellectual as well as moral principle, and be carried from focial intercourfe into the world of thought? He who loves to fee men dwell together in unity muft love to fee related ideas brought together, and may enjoy the meeting of two cognate thoughts that have been kept apart, as much as the meeting of two brothers who have been long feparated. By comparing ifolated ideas, and by tracing out their analogies, new truths are difcovered, and the fatisfaction felt in inferring general principles from particular facts, and in deducing new confequences from familiar axioms, has moft of its warmth and fomething of its origin from the benevolence that delights in difcovering the ties that bind man to man, and man to God. All truths furely are of one family, and God is their father. The good heart helps the believing or truly filial head, and delights to bind together both perfons and principles in faith and love. The bad heart is fceptical in its very felfifhnefs and pafſion, bent on ſundering what God hath joined together.

IV. Moral purity gives life and warmth to the imagination. As imagination is a natural faculty, it is not to be weakened, as ſome ſeem to ſuppoſe, by the proportionate growth of the other powers. The creative power, indeed, muſt take its character and direction from the paſſions and the affections, and love to work upon the materials which they preſent moſt fondly and frequently. When they are in harmony with each other, they produce a ſerenity and cheerfulneſs, that ſhow their fruit in all the creations of the ideal faculty. Poetry never moves men ſo ſtrongly and ſo univerſally as when it comes from warm and healthy affections. The ravings of a diſordered mind, with its mad paſſions, may indeed have a tranſient spell when breathed in the charm of ſweet numbers, and we cannot deny that much poetry has been written by immoral men in deſcription of their peculiar condition with its perverted paſſions and blighted hopes. But upon cloſer analyſis we ſhall find that the great paſſages that have made our profligate claſs of poets illuſtrious, have been thoſe in which they have lamented inſtead of juſtifying their profligacy, and like Burns and Byron, they have brought rich tributes to virtue in penitence from the dark caves of ſenſualiſm. The greateſt poets have, however, lived habitually in the pure air and clear light of Heaven, and ſuch maſters of ſong as Homer, Dante, and Milton, are proof enough that the true inſpiration does not come from any infernal fires or maddening elixirs. They prove that virtue and poetry are natural friends, and that the ideal world opens its treaſures to the true and reverent ſeeker under a law as ſacred and benign as that which opens the facts and principles of external nature to the naturaliſt and philoſopher. A pure eye beſt ſees the light of the ideal as of the natural world, and a bleſſed equanimity, coming not from the death but from the harmony of the paſſions, and giving calmneſs and health to the creative power, clears the ſoul of all blinding films and humors, and opens boundleſs verities and joys to its gaze, interpreting to us perhaps ſomething of what old Pindar meant when he ſpoke of an immortality without tears.

Such are ſome of the favorable influences which moral excellence exerts upon the intellectual character. The queſtion now readily preſents itſelf, what order of motives beſt ſecures the true harmony of our nature, and enables the heart to do its higheſt work for the head? It is eaſy to ſay what is not the true order, and every ſtudent can teſtify at once that the ſpirit of rivalry is allowed to have far more than its proper ſhare in work of education, to the excluſion of higher motives. Rivalry tends to deſtroy the juſt balance of the mind, and inſtead of preſenting to every feeling and faculty its own appropriate motive, it tends to fever them all with a morbid appetite for diſtinction. It impairs our ſenſe of the intrinſic worth of ſtudy and its objects, and calls attention mainly to a point of expediency. It feeds on the accident, not on the ſubſtance, and forgets the means in the end, and that end a partial if not a falſe one. Now I am aware that rivalry is a natural feeling, but I cannot believe that it is maſter of the whole nature. It is undoubtedly given as a ſalutary ſpur to awaken the higher aſpirations, and was never intended of itſelf to be the commanding motive. All the powers and affections have their rightful deſires, and that is the beſt method of culture that preſents to them all the broadeſt and moſt enduring ſatisfaction. Each orb to its orbit, each faculty to its ſphere, each ſpirit to its object—this is our motto. We believe that academic education needs great reform in this direction, and that inftead of being pufhed on by the goad of harfh emulation, we ought to be brought within the attraction of truth and goodnefs more earneftly and wifely. Fame herfelf, which Burke calls the paffion of noble fouls, is not wholly a celeftial. Though her head is among the clouds, and she is ever pointing to the ftars, fhe has made many a man grovel in the duft. But this other fpirit, this reftlefs emulation, has ftill lefs of heaven in her make, and fometimes feems to be at least coufin to the Envy that is born of hell. To look for future name may make a man far-fighted and felf-denying, but the rivalry that is conftantly ftraining for immediate effect has no fuch generous elements, and tends to make its victim the flave of the hour, in fact to break up the integrity of education, and build flafhy little bowers for the paffing feafon, inftead of the fubftantial houfe that refts upon a rock and outlives the ftorm. We muft not indeed demand perfection, and muft be willing, for a time at leaft, to have fome mixture in our motives, but it is not well to think more of the alloy than of the gold. It feems to be as abfurd to fever youth with felfifh emulation, and then tell them that rational ambition will lead to virtue and knowledge, as to place them in the midſt of ſeducing pleaſures, and then ſay that true pleaſure is found only in rectitude.

A paſſage from Lord Bacon is a good interpretation of the ſentence from Juvenal with which I introduced this addreſs: "It may be truly affirmed, that no kind of men love buſineſs for itſelf, but thoſe that are learned; for other perſons love it for profit; as an hireling that loves the work for the wages; or for honor, becauſe it beareth them up in the eyes of men, and refreſheth their reputation, which otherwiſe would wear; or becauſe it exerciſeth ſome faculty wherein they take pride, and ſo entertaineth them in good humor and pleaſing conceits towards themſelves; or becauſe it advanceth any other of their ends. So that as it is ſaid of untrue valors, that ſome men's valors are in the eyes of them that look on; ſo moſt men's induſtries are in the eyes of others or at leaſt in regard of their own deſignments; only the learned love buſineſs as an action according to nature, as agreeable to health of mind as exerciſe is to health of body, taking pleaſure in the action itſelf and not in the purchaſe."

When this principle is applied to ſtudy, a new age will come in education as marked as that age of liberty which this birthnight of Waſhington commemorates. Our ſchools and colleges taking the ſoul's native faculties for the material, and their true proportions for the model, ſhall give each part its due ſtrength, and the whole man his due life and force.

IX.

THE CONDUCT OF LIFE.

FROM THE CLASS ORATION OF JULY 17, 1832.

THAT is perhaps a narrow, though natural principle of aſſociation, that identifies thoughts and feelings with events and places. Surely all that we have been attached to here is ſo cloſely interwoven with theſe familiar ſcenes, that we ſeem in quitting the one to loſe the other. To think of ſo many things that are paſſing away, of the changes in human life, the decay in nature, the ruins of human art, is ever ſaddening. But there is a comfort in remembering that change is not deſtruction. The genius that preſides over all viciſſitude is not a terrible demon, armed with the lightning, robed in the ſtorm, and turbaned with the whirlwind, but a good angel with various and inexhauſtible charms, enlivening the vigils and quickening the ſtrength of the undying ſpirit. The changes which the world conſtantly unfolds to us are hiſtory, and hiſtory is knowledge. The changes in the mind's own life ought to be its progreſs; what is fleeting it ought to fix, and what is periſhable it ought to immortalize. Keats well ſays:

> "A thing of beauty is a joy for ever:
> Its lovelineſs increaſes: * * *
> Therefore every morrow are we wreathing
> A flowery band to bind us to the earth."

So may it be, Claſſmates, with the things that have been pleaſant to us here.

I have ſpoken of the aſſociations of our college life, and the extent and characteriſtics of our culture here, and it is now time to ſpeak of our opening future and the true conduct of life. Whatever good or ill we have laid up for ourſelves, we enter now as we are upon a new life, and we cannot but look forward with eager anticipation. Dreams of happineſs we may indulge at liberty, but plans of life, how little can we ſhape them. We have all had experience enough of men and events to know what power accident has over human conditions. We can feel the truth of the beautiful remark of Goethe when he ſays: "The ſun-horſes of Time, as drawn by unſeen ſpirits, bear away the light chariot of our deſtiny; and nothing remains for us but with tranquil courage to hold firm the reins, and now to the right and now the left, here from a ſtone and there from a precipice, to turn away the wheels. Whither it goes who can tell?" Whither our courſe leads who can tell? We paſs gradually from point to point, and ſeem to guide our courſe. Event ſucceeds event naturally, motive ſprings from motive regularly, thought follows thought rationally. Yet when one compares different ſtages of his career, he is aſtounded at himſelf as at a ſtranger. If four years ago when we came together here, the Book of Time had been opened to us ſo as to ſhow us what we have become now under the action of circumſtances, ideas, aſſociations, and impulſes, who of us would have known himſelf in the deſcription? Yet, much as we are the ſport of chance, the creatures of accident, we are not wholly ſo, and ought to be far leſs so. The fataliſt refutes his own theory by trying to propagate his own ſyſtem. He refutes it more effectively who goes bravely on his determined way, in ſpite of threats and enticements, equal to either fortune, and ſaying, like the old Roman, "Nave ferar magna an parva, ferar unus et idem." He can say to misfortune, like Æneas to the Sibyl:

> "Non ulla laborum
> O Virgo, nova mi facies, inopinave surgit;
> Omnia percepi, atque animo mecum ante peregi."

There is nothing that so fixes a man's attention upon the things of earth, while it lifts him above its ills, as that habit of generalizing peculiar to the liberal scholar and the good man, which forms principles and elevated opinions. The votary of truth who is constantly rising from lower to higher—from finite to infinite, is too free from vulgar prejudices to lose sight of the individual in contemplating what is general. The more he is possessed by the beautiful and the true, the higher he rises in the region of truth, the greater will be his interest in the world and in men, where are the phenomena which started and regulate his speculations. The farther he climbs towards heaven the more earnestly will he regard earth, where the ladder-foot rests. It is no mark of the scholar to neglect the active duties of life, to despise truth in its especial application as trifling, because he has been wont to deal in it largely. Nature knows no trifles. The fall of a leaf and the roll of a planet depend on the ſame law. So it is characteriſtic of a man of high thought to go about among men, obſerve human feeling and help human infirmities—to attach an importance to thoſe things which, neglected as trifles, cauſe moſt of human miſery. He gives everything a dignity in the vital principles it depends upon; ready for every good enterpriſe, deſpiſing not the humble and fearing not the lofty, he will come off conqueror in every undertaking.

The noiſe and buſtle of the world, the cares and troubles of active life, have been the theme of much bugbear eloquence. Noiſy, trouble-finding men are pointed out in proof that little ſhould be hereafter expected but to be joſtled by the motley throng of men, and to be toſſed about on the fickle tide of circumſtances. But it is a comfort to look out into ſociety and ſee that thoſe men who think moſt and accompliſh moſt are they who take life methodically, who live in the trueſt tranquillity, and enjoy the beſt leiſure hours. The greater part of your hurrying buſtling characters, while they make as much noiſe as if they were moving mountains, really effect little. Deliberate and effectual action is not loud and haraſſing. The fertilizing ſtream does not proclaim its flow by its roaring, but by the ſilent yet eloquent verdure that grows round its banks. So magnified have been the vexations, and ſo diſtorted the picture of active life, that it is not an uncommon notion that every one in beginning to act for himſelf muſt muſter a good portion of a certain mountebank boldneſs, which ſome call confidence, but which wiſdom ſeems to rank as akin to impudence. Lord Bacon's conſolation and warranty of ſucceſs to thoſe who ſeek this quality, viz. "that there is in human nature generally more of the fool than the wiſe," ſhould be enough to frighten any man from ſeeking it who has ever breathed an atmoſphere at all impregnated with literary refinement. A view of the beſt and moſt influential perſons in every rank of ſociety, fully proves that a career of manly and unaſſuming effort will be crowned with nobleſt ſucceſs. It is a poor notion to ſuppoſe that life is a continued ſtruggle—a fight for certain good things; to be paſſed beſt it muſt be paſſed in peace, not indeed in that idleneſs which is equally laborious and inefficient—not in that lazy eaſe of temperament, before which thoughts and events float unheeded like the ſhadows of an after-dinner viſion, and which takes from one all claims to an aſtual exiſtence—but in an aſtive, peaceful ſerenity of mind like the fair weather, when buſineſs and nature moſt flouriſh—when the world is fulleſt of aſtion. Such is no monotonous exiſtence; it allows the ſpirits to riſe high in rapture or glide on gently; but it will not allow their clearneſs to be diſturbed by any of "the mud and ooze of Acheron."

This is certainly a very accommodating world. It ſuits every one to what he is looking after. He who ſearches after miſery will be ſure to find it: to him each joy is but the gaudy herald of ſome grief, each ſmile wears the furrow for a future tear—among men he will find enough of evil, and in life enough of the bitter. But if he would find good and happineſs about him—if he would perſuade himſelf that all in the end will be well, with him all will be well: he will not look upon miſery in deſpair, nor turn away from vice in ſelf-righteous abhorrence. God, he will remember, has with his own image ſtamped all men brothers, and demands of him fellow feeling and help: in the midſt of human corruption he will be gladdened and ſtimulated with the thought of what every fellow-being can be: and he will liſten more fondly to the voice that promiſes mercy and joy as troubles and dangers thicken around. What in others kindles the burning fires of anguiſh, in him goes to enlarge and brighten hope's glimmering ray. Anticipation of difficulties and afflictions begins in the very effort to avoid them. One may think deeply upon what he has experienced, and upon the nature of his own mind—he may explore the univerſe to learn the end of his being, till, as it was with Harold, his brain becomes a whirling gulf of phantaſy and flame: yet his philoſophy will not lift him above the man of ſimple faith in the univerſal good, whom partial and proud knowledge has not enticed away into error, and tempted him to ſeek happineſs abroad, where it is not to be found. That is the ſimpleſt as well as the wiſeſt doctrine, which teaches, that now is the accepted time—that now and here are the time and place for happineſs to begin, and puts bliſs in action itſelf not ſolely in its ends.

Much, Claſſmates, that ſhould not be forgotten, has taken place around us and within us during our intercourſe together. While we go to engage in new purſuits and ſeek new ſources of ſatisfaction, may we remember and retain the good we have enjoyed with each other. If buſineſs be ſuffered to engroſs and narrow the mind, if ſelfiſh care be permitted to wither the affections (for there can be no old age of the affections but to the ſelfiſh), the thoughts of old times will bring no pleaſure, the heart will not beat true to the fellowſhip it once loved. The waſte of feelings unemployed—the decay of affection will ſeem like a beginning death —as if the right hand were felt no longer to hold the life-giving tides, no longer reſponded to the touch the ſympathetic glow.

But if we are true to ourſelves, if we keep a warm heart for a friend, and a ready hand for the ſuffering, what has here been pleaſant to us will not paſs away. Then thoughts of the paſt will float bliſsfully along, as ſweet gales from youth's roſy bowers—

> "The weary ſoul will ſeem to ſoothe,
> And redolent of joy and youth
> To breathe a ſecond ſpring."

And now, Claſſmates, here met and here parting we may bid each other an affectionate adieu, and in the farewell words of that rich and genial ſoul, Jean Paul Richter, be this the laſt wiſh of each to all whether preſent or abſent: "May all go well with you—may life's ſhort day glide on peaceful and bright, with no more clouds than may gliſten in the ſunlight, no more rain than may form a rainbow—and may the Veiled One of Heaven watch over your ſteps and bring us to meet again."

X.

OUR SILVER FESTIVAL.

ADDRESS AT THE MEETING OF THE CLASS OF 1832, TWENTY-FIVE YEARS AFTER GRADUATING, JULY 15, 1857.

Classmates—It is a very ſerious date in our life-time that calls us together now, yet the occaſion throws no gloom upon our faces, and opens many old ſprings of joy in our hearts. It is not eaſy to believe it, but true it is that we have been twenty-five years out of College, and that we who ſupped together on Claſs Day, July 17, 1832, a band of merry youths of twenty years or thereabouts, now meet here, after a quarter of a century, to ſup again, with many marks of care upon our features, and more grey hairs in our heads than we are able to count. Yet we feel young to-night, and we invite grim Father Time to lay aſide his ſcythe, and feaſt with us, as he uſed to do long, long ago, when he met with us in youth's genial bowers, and ſmiled with us on the roſes that he meant to cut down and carry away if he could. The beſt bloom, however, he cannot harm; and what was deepeſt and trueſt in the old good fellowſhip blooms out upon us here. We touch a taliſman here that always brings ſpring-time to the affections—a taliſman that is the beſt *tranſmittendum* of the old College, and which has paſſed from generation to generation within the walls of Harvard for centuries, and which will live when ſuch old heirlooms as the "Mathematical Slate" and the "Thundering Bolus" are forgotten. The taliſman is the cup of Youth, the cryſtal goblet graven over with all the names that we have loved, and filled from the affluence of that "vine which bears the wine of life, the human heart." We take this to our lips to-night, and years diſappear, and the youth that is ideal and immortal within the ſoul is ours. Why is it that the long interval ſince we graduated ſeems now ſo ſhort? Is it not in part from the fact that whatever is monotonous and drudging in life, however long and weary in paſſing, ſeems ſhort in retroſpect, from lack of ſalient points; whilſt the happier portion of our experience has been ſo various with kind affections and bright thoughts, as to cheer us with pleaſant viſtas that are too charming to ſeem lengthened; and thus the winning picture of our joys throws into the background the landmarks of our grief and diſappointments, as mountain peaks flaſhing in ſunlight riſe above the long and weary roads? Does not the interval alſo ſeem ſhort becauſe no portion of our life is ſo deeply marked upon us as our youth; and we middle-aged men, with ſome little inclination towards the ſhady ſide of the hill, ſeem to ourſelves and to each other what we uſed to be; and as we meet together here we are boys once more—old boys, perhaps, yet boys indeed. We are to each other like palimpſeſt manuſcripts to the practiſed ſcholar. The world has been writing many inſcriptions upon us, yet the firſt is deepeſt and ineffaceable; and beneath all theſe marks of time and care we can read the dear old cypher of our early love and joy. To each other we ſeem not as we do to the world, and to us the words and looks and air that the crowd do not notice open whole volumes of remembrance.

OUR CLASS.

It was my lot to give the Claſs Oration in 1832, and this fact has probably led the Claſs Committee, with the concurrence of an informal meeting laſt year, to aſk me to write ſomething for this meeting of the claſs. I would cheerfully take any needed pains to fulfil the duty properly, yet it has ſeemed to me not ſo well to give an elaborate oration on ſome literary ſubject at this ſeaſon, when orations are a deluge and rhetoric is a drug, as to give ſome familiar reminiſcences that may ſerve as a memorial of our claſs. To ourſelves this occaſion belongs, and let "Our Claſs" be the ſubject. To us "Our Claſs" is *the* one claſs; and without aſking others to ſhare the feeling, we will take it for granted, as all lovers and friends do, that we are eſpecially intereſting to ourſelves, and that we can goſſip about ourſelves none the leſs pleaſantly becauſe we do not now care one ſtraw whether other people are thinking of us or not. Since the year 1642 a claſs has annually graduated from Harvard, with the exception of five years, or 1644–48–72–82–88, ſo that 210 ſets of graduates call old Harvard their mother, and each ſet in its own way has kept up more or leſs of claſs feeling. All honor to the other 209 claſſes, from the year 1642 to 1857. All honor to their members, living or dead. Yet, taking the ſame liberty that we reſpect in them, we ſtand up for our own good fellows, and the Claſs of 1832 is Our Claſs.

I ſuppoſe that each claſs has ſomething peculiar in its compoſition and hiſtory, and that without arrogance we may claim a certain ſpeciality to ourſelves. We entered college at a marked time, and had characteriſtics quite our own. In our Freſhman year Preſident Quincy was inaugurated, and his adminiſtration began a new era in the college annals, by bringing into its financial management more ſecular enterpriſe, and connecting with the eſtabliſhed round of claſſic ſtudies more of the ſcience and art that are concerned with the world's daily buſineſs. If in our new preſident we miſſed ſomething of the evangelical ſimplicity and paſtoral affectionateneſs ſo characteriſtic of the long line of clerical Preſidents, we found in him great energy in affairs, and far leſs of the hardneſs of the magiſtrate in dealing out diſcipline to acknowledged offenders, than the ſagacity of the ſtateſman in ferreting out the offence. Sometimes he could, perhaps, have won us more heartily to ſtudy and obedience by appealing more to our enthuſiaſm and good will; but we have all now learned to look to him as a father, and we had in our Preſident a magnificent example of manly energy and health, of public ſpirit, which made our welfare his own, and of ſterling humanity, which has never given better proof of itſelf than in his old age, ſo ſacred to the liberty and order that have always been deareſt to the true ſons of Harvard from the beginning. Honor, all honor to Quincy, now *Old* Quincy, in the ſacred ſenſe which no naughty Sophomore would dare to name with levity. In having him for our Preſident, we did not loſe good old Dr. Ware, who had preſided till the cloſe of our Freſhman year, and who preached and prayed for us afterwards, as before, nurturing in us the love of all good men, whatever be their creed, and in the pulpit and the recitation-room, alike by the ſhake of his head and the balance of his opinions, ſymbolizing his characteriſtic deſire to appreciate all ſides of a queſtion, and to be juſt to every man. Peace to his ſpirit! The memory of the juſt is bleſſed.

THE RAW MATERIAL IN 1828.

To write the hiſtory of Our Claſs from the firſt to the laſt of our undergraduate days, would be nothing lefs than to write out the characters that we brought with us to College, and the influences that acted upon us there, or to defcribe our feveral individualities, that were the raw material, and the College experiences that worked us into fhape. This tafk I will not attempt, but muft be content with a paffing glance at ourfelves and at our fofter mother in our days of tutelage. We were feventy-two ftrong on entering College; and if any of us ever need an illuftration of the boundlefs variety of the human race, whether in looks, talent, or difpofition, let him remember the *men* of our clafs—*men*, I fay, for we were all more eager to be called fo when Frefhmen, and hardly efcaped the days of fhort jackets, than when Seniors, and frightened at the refponfibilities which go in the train of "fwallow-tails." We were in fome refpects known, and in fome refpects unknown quantities. Part of our nature was like the *a b c* of mathematics, amply defined, whilft another part was like the unknown *x y z*, whofe fignificance was to be defined by folving the problem of life in the fchool of books and experience. As we look back upon ourfelves as we were in 1828, when we entered College, thefe unknown quantities appear to us as then they could not appear, and the great revelations of life have been developing the unknown from the known. We were of all ages, from 14 to 24; of all ſizes, from little F. and B. to big R. and D.; of all complexions, from cherry-cheeked boys, with chins as ſmooth as their ſiſters', to ſwarthy men, with beards like pards; of all expreſſions, from the humorous face, that was in itſelf a ſong or joke, to the ſerious viſage, that was fit promiſe of a ſermon, and a good ſermon, too; of all fancies, from the ſloven, who preferred a dirty ſhirt to a clean one, to the born dandy, on whom an old coat looked as good as new; of all taſtes, from him who organized the Smoking Club, to him who organized a prayer-meeting; of all talents, from him who gave practical illuſtrations of the law of exploſives, as if to aſcertain how the world would be moſt effectually deſtroyed, to him who devoted himſelf, not without good ſucceſs, to the moral inſtruction and reform of us all, with the hope of building up the New Jeruſalem out of ſuch heterogeneous materials. In fact, thoſe ſeventy-two youths were a univerſity in themſelves; and by clubbing our various gifts together, we might have undertaken in due time to perform almoſt any given taſk, whether in language, literature, mathematics, ſcience, art, uſeful or beautiful, proſaic or poetic, mechanical or muſical, tragic or comic, in ethics, metaphyſics, or theology. We were, indeed, put generally upon nearly the ſame courſe of ſtudies; yet we very ſoon ſhowed our individual preferences for favorite branches; whilſt a few, with ſingular independence of mind, exhibited decided averſion to all the regular ſtudies, and fell back upon our primeval inſtincts and intuitions, with an utter contempt for academic diplomas. It would be an intereſting matter to trace out the effect of our previous ſchooling and aſſociations upon our College ſtudies and habits. With ſome of us cliques and taſtes came with us to College that remained with us during the whole four years, and have not left us yet. Such aſſociations as are formed in boyhood cannot but act upon youth; and probably the Boſton and Salem influence was a great element in our claſs. Boſton, from its Latin ſchool, ſent a hoſt, headed by J. S. D., whoſe face here to-night keeps all the ideal promiſe of its genial prime; and Salem ſent almoſt a ſcore, headed by C. T. B., the claſs pet, and to-night our poet, whom all our petting, inſtead of ſpoiling, makes more lovable than ever. Other places contributed memorably to our variety of character and ſcholarſhip, but of these various cliques, of the many individualities that brought to us the idioſyncraſies of quiet homes and lonely ſtudies, I cannot treat in detail.

The dividing line between mental aptitudes is probably drawn at firſt more decidedly by the predilection either for language or mathematics than by any other teſts, although a few minds excel in both; and in the later ſeaſon of college life a ſomewhat ſimilar line is drawn between phyſics and metaphyſics. As a claſs we were probably more marked for our taſte for language and literature, and at laſt for metaphyſics, than for mathematics and exact ſcience. We ſtudied the Latin and Greek quite tolerably, and not a few were willing to make pedeſtrian journeys into the claſſic regions without the help of horſe or pony, whilſt we carried a decided enthuſiaſm into the modern languages, and perhaps made a new era in the academic ſtudy of German. With us, I believe, the ſtudy of the Portugueſe at Cambridge originated, and Dr. Bachi certainly dedicated his Portugueſe Grammar to the little band of claſſmates who ſtudied with him the great epic of Camoens. There was, indeed, a decidedly philoſophical tendency in our claſs, but it was given more fondly to moral and metaphyfical than to mathematical or fcientific fubjects. Even the more fcientific minds of the clafs took more to practical fubjects, fuch as natural hiftory, electricity, and the like, than to abftract fcience; and far more volunteer zeal was given to infects, frogs, and magnets, than to the calculus and eclipfes. The higher mathematics, indeed, had enthufiaftic votaries among us, and the auguft miffion of all the exact fciences was acknowledged in our ftudies and debates, yet our clafs fpecialities were not mainly in that direction.

OUR TEACHERS.

We had, on the whole, an excellent corps of teachers to reprefent the magnificent treafure of humanities confided to the keeping of the Univerfity, and their names fpeak volumes of experience more or lefs favored. The chief and moft of them have gone, and of thefe we think only tenderly, grateful for what they did for us and bore with in us; too grateful for their good fervice to be fevere upon their infirmities, if fuch they had. Hedge, Willard, Ware, Channing, Popkin, Follen, Sales,

Bachi, Farrar, Nuttall, and others have paſſed away, whilſt others who taught us have gone into other profeſſions or retired into private life, such as Tick-nor, Giles, Hillard, Sweetſer, Beck. Only two of the old academic corps now remain, and our old tutors, Felton and Pierce, now head the liſt of pro-feſſors, fit interpreters of Homer and Newton ſtill. We owe ſomething to all our teachers, and much to moſt of them. We all learned not a little under their inſtruction, and might have learned a great deal more, if we had made better uſe of our time and opportunities. Yet in juſtice we may make two remarks as to the bearings of the ſtated inſtruc-tion upon our ſtudy and character. In the firſt place, we may juſtly regret that more was not done to quicken our own minds by the teacher's perſonal influence, inſtead of confining us ſo excluſively to the formal recitation of the contents of the text-books; and, moreover, that in addition to the teachers of ſpecial branches, there was not ſome general ſuperintendent or adviſer to watch over the progreſs and defects of our general culture, and give us wholeſome hints as to the way of making the beſt uſe of ourſelves for the College term and for the great lifework. It may alſo be ſaid with entire juſtice that, much as was done to educate us, we did a great deal to educate ourſelves, and that no portion of our college experience has been of more practical value to us than that which we worked out for ourſelves. In fact, the formation of character, which is a more vital matter than the acquiſition of knowledge, depends chiefly upon the influence of companions upon each other; and, from the firſt, by our manly ſports and our good fellowſhip, our cenſures and favor, we were doing much to ſhape our diſpoſitions and purpoſes. Undoubted good came from ſome colliſions that were painful to us at firſt, and thoſe of us who came from retired homes, the timid pets of fond kindred and friends, have cauſe to be grateful that ſo much nonſenſe was taken out of us by practical jokes and rough ſports that are now more pleaſant in remembrance than in the time of our perhaps tearful experience. But we, as a claſs, were remarkable for perſiſtent and ſomewhat ſyſtematic methods of acting upon each other. The faculty more important than any other to the public men of America, the faculty of extempore ſpeaking, was regularly cultivated by voluntary ſocieties; and in addition to the old line of eſtabliſhed inſtitutions, we ſtarted one of our own, the Harvard Union, which was open to all who ſought its privileges, and which abounded in debaters and debates that were the talk of the whole college, and whoſe influence many of us have had cauſe to bleſs throughout our whole profeſſional life. Not a few amuſing reminiſcences ſtart up at the name of Harvard Union, and none of us can forget the ſtudied efflореſcence of one ambitious aſpirant for the rhetorical palm, and the unbounded admiration with which the ſomewhat jocoſe grandiloquence of our handſome claſſmate T., which was received with a good-natured ſmile by moſt of us, was greeted by one enthuſiaſtic hearer, who predicted for the orator the firſt prizes of popular favor. In one ſenſe, at leaſt, the prophecy is correct; and if the largeſt letters on the Catalogue imply the largeſt fame, our friend T. has won the palm. With theſe regular debates we name the informal talks and diſcuſſions that were ſo frequent in our rambles and in our rooms, upon ſubjects of all ſorts, but tending decidedly towards the higher queſtions of human duty and deſtiny. We value theſe converſations for their occaſional fun as well as for their frequent ſeriouſneſs; and I really believe that whilſt we owe much to the thoughtful men who turned our minds ſo often to high moral and religious topics, we are alſo much indebted to the funny men who ſhook the dyſpepſia out of us, by ſhaking our diaphragms with wholeſome laughter, and helped us purge our faith of the too frequent cant by their genial humor. For one, I am very grateful to the comedians of our claſs, and I verily believe that their merry ſongs and ſtories were moſt valuable ſanatives to body and to mind.

CATHOLICITY.

One trait in the character of our claſs is eſpecially noteworthy. We had one kind of fraternal largeneſs or catholicity that is not uſual in college—a catholicity that was willing to allow every man the liberty of his own honeſt opinions, and not diſpoſed to force its own ſtandard of ſtrictneſs or freedom upon all others. With us this liberty took a peculiar form, from the predominance of claſſmates deſtined for the clerical profeſſion. Theſe minds, from their number and character, were probably more influential than any other portion of the claſs, and they received cordially from others a decided encouragement, not general in undergraduate life, to ſpeak out their convictions frankly and fully, without being ſneered at or diſparaged in any way. As one of thoſe who early made choice of the clerical profeſſion, I muſt expreſs gratitude to the claſs for their treatment of us, not only for not diſparaging a profeſſion that ſeems uſually more ſpectral than ſpiritual to gay youth, but for not being unmerciful towards the perſonal failings, of which ſome of us were not unconſcious, and which needed much diſcipline to prevent them from interfering with the proper ſpirit of our choſen calling. If the theological portion of the claſs have cauſe of gratitude for ſuch toleration and forbearance, it muſt be remembered that, with hardly an exception, they tried to deſerve it by their own candor and charity. They tried to have religion without cant or auſterity, and were generally too conſcious of their own defects to be unſparing in cenſure of the errors of others. The catholicity thus ſhown in one direction was quite general in its application, and it is a very pleaſant thing to remember the various taſtes and talents that had their accredited repreſentatives among us, and the many lines of ſpecial ſtudy not demanded by the college ſyſtem, but which won for the adepts in them quite as much reſpect from us as for the ftudies that decided the fcale of college rank. That fcale was never popular with us, partly becaufe unmindful of fuch fpecialities. Almoft every claffmate had fomething noteworthy, and the trite *E Pluribus Unum*, by which General Jackfon is faid to have won his LL.D. from our hofpitable Alma Mater, was well illuftrated in the unity and the variety of our clafs. From many we were and are one, and never was the fact more clear than from this genial meeting of all profeffions to-night.

CHANGES IN COLLEGE LIFE.

We changed much alike in members and in development of character during our undergraduate years. A confiderable number left us, and more joined us. Of thofe who left us, fix were removed by death, and their names fhould be fpoken of affectionately here to-night—Bradford, Hodges, Peters, Rantoul, Treadwell, Welch. Each of thefe might fitly have a fpecial word; but I name particularly the two who were in our fection—Peters, a man of confiderable humor, great fhrewdnefs, and with not a little genuine fellowfhip under his awkward exterior; and Rantoul, a quiet, fenfible, genial, lovable fellow, whoſe lameneſs ſeemed to ſweeten inſtead of ſouring him, and who made up by the playful freedom of his tongue for the want of as ready locomotion in his limbs. He was a quiet and kindly philoſopher in his way, and not inaptly called "Cool Sam." Theſe, and the whole ſix who died before we graduated, we remember as part of ourſelves.

The changes in developments of character were quite memorable during our four years together. This lapſe of time, at that ſeaſon of life, is marked in the phyſical conſtitution by making men of boys, and it is quite as decidedly marked by its tranſition from boyiſh gaiety to manly thoughtfulneſs. There were great differences in the uſe made by different claſſmates of their time and talents, and there is probably not one of us who does not regret ſomething that he did or failed to do in college. But on the whole, as a claſs, we vaſtly improved, and a practical, earneſt, manly ſpirit won more and more power over us as the years went on. Undoubtedly there was much in our experience which we each kept to ourſelves—some pinches of hard fortune, fits of gloom, aſſaults of temptation, guſts of paſſion, as well as viſitations of interior peace—that we did not care to tell to others. Yet in the main we were a tranſparent ſet of fellows, and probably knew each other's failings and virtues tolerably well; and we found enough of the bright ſide predominating to make us like each other better than is uſual with comrades of a four years' voyage, and to part in hearty good will, with hope of many genial reunions. We ſang "Auld Lang Syne" together as we parted; and if there was or has been ſince any bad blood between any of our claſſmates, or if there was any ſuch then, I have not known it, and am ſure that no bad blood beats in any of our hearts as we ſing that good old ſong to-night.

THE TWENTY-FIVE YEARS SINCE GRADUATING.

And now, claſſmates, here we are, after twenty-five years of our graduation—years given to very different purſuits, and demanding very different labors from thoſe of our college courſe. We have had to ſtudy, not text-books, but men and things—thoſe volumes that are always changing, never complete, and as ſcattered and fragmentary, yet as full of meaning, as the Sybil's leaves. We have had to ſtudy theſe, moreover, not ſo much with a ready memory and a glib tongue, as with practical ſenſe and energetic will. It was a hard ordeal to go through in this tranſition; and ſome, who were good recitation ſcholars, did not ſtand ſo well the world's ſtern croſs-queſtions, and found that many important leſſons had to be learned over again. Probably all of us ſuffered much in beginning the world for ourſelves, and we found the water colder than we expected before we took the plunge. Yet the reäction was equal to the action, if we only had ſtrength to bear it, and our beſt experience has come to us in the ſchool of practical uſefulneſs. Many things have proved otherwiſe than we thought, and probably moſt of us have had diſappointments, both agreeable and diſagreeable, as affairs have gone better or worſe than we expected. There have been in both directions unlooked for developments of character and fortune, as we have compared reſults with early promiſes. It is clear to us that force of character has done for our men more than mere book-learning, and that life is not graduated on the ſcale of academic rank. It is clear that circumſtance is a mighty element in ſucceſs, and that the men who have had the moſt brilliant career will be the laſt to claim to themſelves all the honor for opportunities denied to other men as deſerving as themſelves. Our claſs has furniſhed its fair ſhare of notables, whether uſeful or ornamental; its lawyers, doctors, clergymen, merchants, farmers, naturaliſts, poets, authors, critics, editors, profeſſors, lecturers, and judges. Perhaps ſome of our men who are leaſt conſpicuous have had their full ſhare of ſucceſs, in the large meaſure of real good that they have enjoyed and helped others to enjoy. Of the conſiderable number who have died during the quarter century, moſt of them had as good a proſpect of health and life as we, the ſurvivors; and as we name their names,* we cannot but think tenderly of them, as having been ſtruck by the fatal ſhafts to which we were all expoſed, and fallen, perhaps, in our ſtead. It is quite remarkable that our moſt robuſt claſſmate, Huntington, was firſt to die. Of the dead of our claſs, ſome of conſpicuous mark quite ſurpriſed our expectation either by developments of character or poſition; and it is not invidious to name two whoſe career was little in accordance with their early promiſe.

* Adams 1, Adams 2, Cleveland, Glover, Gibbs, Huntington, Liggett, Manning, Pentland, Perkins, Phipps, Ropes, Richardſon, Simmons, Stark, Walker, Weſt, Worceſter.

One of the moſt jocoſe, elaſtic of the whole claſs—a character of whom I could tell many amuſing ſtories—fell a victim to melancholy; and although maſter of wealth, had at laſt little ability to enjoy it. We may remember affectionately his great contributions to our amuſement and our good fellowſhip, and over his grave learn anew our dependence upon health for good ſpirits, whilſt we pray to be ſpared the malady that wrecked his joy. The other claſſmate to be named is he who, of all the others, had promiſe of the moſt brilliant career. He was preëminently our beſt ſpeaker, as well as a fine ſcholar and an exquiſite writer; and if the general vote of our thoughtful men had been taken at graduating, the moſt ſhining career, as a public ſpeaker, would have been aſſigned to Simmons. He had ſucceſs, indeed, the beſt ſucceſs, that of a true man, ſincere, profound, humane, and devout; and he whoſe ſomewhat crabbed temper and conſtitutional reſerve ſometimes diſpleaſed us, deſerves the name of ſaintly piety and ſelf-ſacrificing virtue as much as any man of our fellowſhip. Yet he did not ſucceed, as was expected, in popular oratory and public fame. Perhaps the cauſe of his comparative ineffectiveneſs was partly in the want of ſocial ſympathy that we noted of old; and in life, as in College, he failed to touch the hearts of the many, becauſe more engroſſed with abſtract thoughts and individual experiences, than in ſympathy with the common affections and convictions of men, and living in a world of his own quite as much when ſpeaking and talking to the people as in his own private walk or ſtudy. Yet upon not a few who knew him beſt, he had great and good influence, and by his beſt friends no man among us was more revered than he. I name him affectionately and gratefully to-night. He did much for us all in college by his beautiful elocution, exquiſite taſte, and ſpotleſs character. In after years, we, who knew him ſocially and profeſſionally, honored him as never before. Two years ago, a few weeks before his death, I met him on his ſlow and painful journey homeward towards Concord, and joined another friend in carrying Simmons in our arms from the ſtation to the cars, the once ſtout and elaſtic frame, ſtronger than mine, now feeble as a child's. His ſucceſs was not of this world's giving, and of him we may ſay tenderly and humbly, as we compare his rewards with his merits, "The race is not to the ſwift, nor the battle to the ſtrong, nor riches to men of underſtanding." Peace be with him, and with all who with him have gone from us to the unſeen abodes.

THE FUTURE.

And now, claſſmates, it is time to cloſe theſe curſory retroſpections, and let our paſt ſpeak for itſelf in our preſent fellowſhip. Twenty-five years have gone, and taken with them moſt of the ſtruggle and opportunity of our earthly career. Fifty years after graduating is as long a leaſe of life as any of us may expect, and more than any conſiderable number of us can have. Half of that fifty years has paſſed, and the ſecond half brings us to or beyond the threeſcore and ten allotted to man. Let us not mourn over this inevitable neceſſity, but thank God for the good that we have enjoyed, and not doubt that more good is in ſtore for us and for all dear to us. Thank God that we have enjoyed ſo much together for the twenty-nine years ſince we firſt met as ſchoolboys, and learned to ſay "Our Claſs." We cannot deny that we have attained a very ſerious age, and many of us have recorded the paſſage of events by witneſſes more living and conſpicuous than the dates of the Catalogue or Claſs-book. Let us not believe, however, that a ſerious age is of neceſſity a gloomy one, but rather take it for granted that the longer we live the better we ought to know how to live, and ſo win the beſt good of nature, man, and God. Our bloſſoming time is paſt, yet even this vernal joy we have anew in our children, for they are our bloſſoms; and, moreover, our true fruit-time has come or is coming —the bleſſed autumn, that is richeſt in deep tints, and precious harveſts, and prophetic hopes. God grant to us an autumn full of fruit fair and nouriſhing, ſo as to take from wintry age its terrors. Let us help each other in this cheerful view, and whenever we meet together, as now, find our wiſdom and ſtrength as much enlarged as our joy. Let us always, as we meet, read over the names of our Catalogue affectionately, noting all good traits generouſly, and treating faults in others as we wiſh our faults to be treated by them. When another twenty-five years have gone, and a little band of ſeptuagenarians gather together to celebrate our Golden Anniverſary, let them ſtand manfully by the old faith and fellowſhip, and pledge each other genially, as we do now:

To our Claſs—to the health of the living—to the memory of the dead—to all of our Claſs,

XI.

PAST AND PRESENT.

FOR THE TWENTY-FIFTH ANNIVERSARY OF THE CLASS (AT HARVARD) OF 1832.

BY REV. C. T. BROOKS.

How beautiful the feet
That, from manhood's duſty track,
To the green and ſhaded ſeat
Of the Muſes haſten back—
To Learning's, Friendſhip's, Memory's honor'd ſhrine!
From the race-ground's heat and toil
How gratefully they turn—
From the battle-ground's turmoil
To thy ſtillneſs how they yearn,
Auld Lang Syne!

Their Delphi's claſſic fount
In thy tranquil realm they find—

Their Zion's hallowed mount—
Their "Mecca of the mind"—
The Sepulchre, the Altar, and the Urn:
Calm and holy is the air—
Fresh and holy is the ground—
Deathless garlands breathe around,
And vigil-torches there
Ever burn.

Thus, Brothers, come we now
Our ancient home to greet,
And, with pensive, reverent brow,
To lay at Wisdom's feet
Our votive gift in Thought's memorial hall:
We heard the ghostly breeze,
With a low-voiced music moan,
Through old Harvard's quivering trees,
And there breathed a mother's tone
In the call.

We come the scenes to trace
Of happy, youthful days—
Each well-remembered place
Of studies, walks, and plays—
But ah, the change! "Ah, fields beloved in vain!"

How near and yet how far
That picture fair doth ſeem!
So ſhines an evening ſtar
With ſoftened ſummer gleam
O'er the plain.

Alas, the fleeting years!
Remembrance! bliſsful pain!
What though thy bitter tears,
Like drops of latter rain,
O'er graves of days and joys departed fall?
On life's autumnal mould—
The duſt of Memory's dead—
The burning tears grow cold;
No ſhower the ſpring that fled
Can recall.

Yet *this* the ſpirit cheers—
This pearl, from dark depths won:—
Though built of memory's tears,
In life's declining ſun,
Fair ſign of Hope an evening rainbow yields.
Though Time may ne'er reſtore
Full many a form and face—
The loved and loſt of yore—
Transfigured, they ſhall grace
Holier fields!

Not gloomy, then, though ſad,
We turn our pilgrim-feet,
With lofty faith made glad,
To this reverend retreat,
Peopled with holy dead, that die no more.
Meet is it, we to-day,
In the world's diſtracting ſtrife,
Should pauſe upon our way,
And the voice of death and life
Ponder o'er.

Five times five years have fled
Since the warm midſummer night,
Now numbered with the dead,
Yet warm in memory's light,
When, with youth's and muſic's wild, commingling swell,
Till the ceiling's echoes rang,
And the agitated air
Made the very tapers flare,
Our laſt vows and hopes we ſang—
And farewell!

And we felt a nameleſs thrill,
As the parting hour drew nigh,

Our eyes and boſoms fill,
When the night-wind's plaintive ſigh
Bore away the dying accents of our chorus:
"We are breaking the laſt ties,—
Brothers, claſſmates, with the dawn
Of the morrow we are gone,
And Life's broad ocean lies
All before us!"

Five times five years have fled—
Summer ſun and winter ſnow
Five and twenty times have ſhed
On the cheek the dark brown glow,
And ſtreaked the hair with lines of ſilver grey—
And a thinned and waſted band,
From the fields and flood of life,
Scathed by ſtorm and ſcarred by ſtrife,
At the trumpet-call we ſtand
Here to-day.

In the claſſic days of yore,
As each fifth year came round,
Her children counting o'er,
Through the cleanſed city's bound
Kept holy time our ancient mother Rome.
With us the faithful ſun,

Commander of the ſphere,
Through luſtrums five hath run,
And this moſt ſolemn year
Calls us home!

We ſeek our boundary-ſtones,
A band of comrades true,
Old Harvard's loyal ſons,
To keep with honors due,
Our year of numbering and of purifying;
To call the blotted roll,
Our miſſing ones to tell,
And mourn for them that fell,
Whoſe memory in the ſoul
Bides undying.

And while the ſtoried wall
Memorial tablets grace,
In thought's heaven-lighted hall
A high and ſacred place
Shall many a *votive* tablet alſo find:
Faith's pious incenſe there
And gratitude's clear fire
Shall purify the air
And from every baſe deſire
Cleanſe the mind.

What mingling ſmiles and tears—
What lights and glooms flit faſt
O'er the picture, as the years
Of the ſlumbering dreamy paſt
From the magic circle ſtart again to life;—
And again, a boyiſh band,
With elaſtic ſtep, we tread
A claſſic, mythic land,
Trained by ſage and hero dead
For the ſtrife!

Alas! no more on earth,
That Friendſhip ſhall be found!
The muſic and the mirth
That charmed for us this ground,
And drew down heaven ſo near us,—all is o'er!
No more, as then, we'll meet
In chamber, hall, or grove,—
No more take counſel ſweet,
Nor in free, fond converſe rove,—
Nevermore!

Another lot was ours,
For *this was not our reſt;*
Not in theſe fading bowers
The ſoul can find her neſt;

Man's Eden lies beyond the bounds of earth.
In this harbor's green retreat
Piped the wind one ſummer-morn,
And, like leaves by whirlwinds torn,
On life's ocean was our fleet
Scattered forth.

And ſome whoſe hopes were high
In that morning's freſhening breeze,
And who ſaw, with kindling eye,
Proud havens o'er the ſeas,
Ere noon have ſunk beneath the "envious ſurge."
The wind that, favoring, blew,
And the trumpet-ſignal gave,
As their pennon ſeaward flew,
Already o'er their grave
Sings the dirge.

And, fellow-pilgrims, ye
Who, ſpared the untimely fate,
Still ride or ſtem the ſea,
Or, in ſome port, await
The ſignal-call of Him who ſits on high,—
Say, does the ſolemn paſt

Sound on in memory's ear
Like Duty's trumpet-blaſt,
With warning and with cheer,
From the ſky?

The paſt, it is not dead—
It lives, in memory, ſtill;
Though the outer form hath fled,
Yet the inner ſenſes thrill
To the viſion and the voice of days gone by.
Gone by? ah no—not gone,
But, like the world of night,
Unſeen in day's bold light,
For ever following on,
Ever nigh.

Our loved and loſt ones riſe
In glory from the duſt,—
The gentle and the wiſe,
The ſaintly and the juſt,
Teacher revered, true friend and truſted guide;
And heavenly is their talk,
And on the tranquil brow
Beams heavenly radiance now,
While, as of old, they talk
At our ſide.

Yes, from its place of old,
Though youth's fair world is gone,
Like morning's web of gold
From the dew-befpangled lawn,
The paft is ours—no more to pafs away—
Its pleafures and its pains,
Each glory and defeat,
Its loffes and its gains,
The bitter and the fweet,
Ours for aye!

Each generous dream of youth
That bade us wage, through life,
For virtue, right, and truth
Heroic, holy ftrife;
Each earneft ftruggle of the better will;
Each heavenly defire,
Each wife and lofty thought,
Each fpark of manly fire
From faint, fage, warrior caught,
Nerves us ftill.

Nor yet with us abide
Thefe angels bright, alone:—
Clofe follow at our fide,
With fad, yet tender tone,

And with reproachful, not reſentful brow,
Scorned Wiſdom, ſlighted Age,
And Time neglected, too,—
Theſe, from a higher page,
Kind monitors and true,
Teach us now.

This moral ends my rhyme:—
Claſſmates who ſtill muſt learn,
In this great ſchool of time,
Full many a leſſon ſtern,—
One Friend—one Teacher—bides when all is paſt.
On Him and for Him wait—
Till, at the ſignal-call,
Through that myſterious gate,
To higher forms we all
Riſe at laſt!

XII.

THE USE OF TIME.

TIME is ſurely one of the chief gifts of man, and the condition of uſing every other rational gift. All his plans are baſed upon its duration, and when he cannot reckon upon the paſt or the future, his world is chaos or his reaſon is gone. We cannot uſe a verb or do a thing without expreſſing or implying the idea of time. Thought itſelf is bound up with that idea, for what is memory without a paſt, and what is judgment without a preſent and future? Time is man's beſt external property, for by its uſe in enterpriſe he wins the beſt external goods, and by its uſe in ſpiritual wiſdom he makes external goods yield laſting harveſts of interior bleſſing. Wiſely ſaid the poet—

> Time is my eſtate, my dukedom is time.

Let us meditate upon this poſſeſſion now. That we may not go aſtray in our views of the true uſe of time let us take a preliminary glance at its nature that we learn at leaſt to note its paſſage wiſely. What is time? Does any one ſay that the queſtion is too ſimple to be aſked, and everybody knows what it is? It is preciſely theſe ſimple queſtions that are hardeſt to anſwer, becauſe they treat of ultimate facts that cannot be ſimplified. One of the deepeſt thinkers, St. Auguſtine, I believe it was, once ſaid, If you do not aſk me what time is, I know; but the moment you aſk me, I know nothing about it. True it is that we have a kind of intuitive ſenſe of time that is diſturbed, like everything intuitive, by attempts to define it. Yet the attempt may remove ſome errors that may ſtand in the way of the intuitive idea.

It is ſurely a great error to confound time itſelf with any choſen meaſure of its duration. We look at the clock and tell the time by its dial to our great convenience. But the hands that tell the hour do not make, but merely meaſure it, and time would paſs on abſolutely the ſame in itſelf, if no clocks had been ever made, or all that have been made ſhould be broken. The cunning mechaniſm but imitates the motion of the great dial of the heavens, and even this dial only meaſures and does not make time. Let the ſun be darkened or let the earth ceaſe her rotation, and ſtill there would be duration of ſome kind, and therefore time. The very fact that things exiſt, and continue either in motion or in reſt, implies duration, and how can there be duration without time?

We are compelled, therefore, to take the ground that time is one of the eſſential facts of exiſtence and forms of thought. What its eſſential nature is we do not preſume to ſay, but are content to leave it among the ultimate truths of exiſtence, where we leave all abſolute ideas. Owning the limitation of our underſtanding in the quarter tranſcending its ſearch, we are all the more ready to uſe it in its rightful ſphere, and to decide upon the true practical meaſure of time. Whatever gives the beſt idea of duration gives us practically the beſt idea of time, and carrying out this principle we add at once an inward meaſure of its paſſage to the uſual outward ſtandard. Not ſatisfied to mark duration by the ſun or the clock, which note the hours alike over a ſterile deſert and a growing garden, or over a beſotted ſluggard and a thoughtful worker, we aſk for ſome better chronicle of what is paſſing under the heavens. What chronicle can we have but that which marks the interior events of exiſtence, and makes the life the light of the world. Aſk ſtill what is the hour of the day, and what things transpire within its period; but aſk alſo what is the hour in the interior kingdom, and what thoughts, affections, purpoſes, make up its moments. Can ye not watch with me one hour, ſaid our Saviour to his diſciples who had fallen aſleep in the garden of his agony. The hour paſſed the ſame indeed, if meaſured by the ſtars, with the maſter and the diſciple; but oh, how different if meaſured by the torpid brain of the wearied ſleeper, and the intenſe ſpiritual life of Him then ſo ſtruggling with the powers of darkneſs and winning angels to his ſide. Learn then to mark time by the current of life as well as by the ſucceſſion of hours. Without the dial, thought may be vague and dreamy for want of a ſpecific meaſure, but without the eſtimate of thought the dial is a ſhallow guide, telling how the ſtream paſſes without telling us the depth of its volume or the wealth within or upon its waters.

"Dark flood of time!
Roll as it liſteth thee. I meaſure not
By months or moments thy ambiguous courſe.
—— The ſenſe of love,

> The thirst for action and the impassioned thought
> Prolong my being: If I wake no more
> My life more actual living will contain
> Than some gray veteran of the world's cold school,
> Where listless hours unprofitably roll
> By one enthusiast feeling unredeemed."

Learning thus to measure time alike by the succession of thought and the passage of hours, we next ask what is the duty of man as a subject of time. It is clear that there must be a specific and important relation between the human constitution and the vast and mysterious element in which it lives and moves. Both sides of our nature are alike concerned in it—both the active and the passive sphere. If time is measured by the succession of things, it calls us either to action or to rest, to work or to wait, according as the succession of things is to be brought to pass by our effort or to come to pass of itself. Here then the two great time-virtues open upon us—enterprise and patience; the one bidding us do what we can to set the times right—the other bidding us abide calmly the times that are beyond our control. He is a wise and strong man who looks well to each duty and uses his time with enterprise and patience.

Who of us can afford to ſlight either of these? What man can afford to be idle and allow his ſacred heritage to run to waſte? Are there not twelve hours in the day, and does not the very light in heaven that marks them off tell us in every gleam, "Work while it is day, for the night cometh when no man can work." Do ſomething every day in the name of Him who loads every hour with opportunity, for the welfare of a world never enough bleſſed with good works, and for the peace of your own mind, which is never ſo happy as in bringing ſome worthy plan to paſs. Without limitation the command to work is binding upon us. We have not all the ſame work to do, but we all have ſome work, and a curſe is upon us when we try to repudiate it. No perſon has a right to be idle before God. If a man has ample means and leiſure to withdraw from the general buſineſs of the world, as is the caſe with ſome privileged perſons, it is well if he uſes his exemption from taſk-labor to occupy his time with purſuits congenial with his taſtes. But the moment he gives up any kind of conſcientious and ſyſtematic exertion and becomes a merely paſſive dependent upon external excitement, he is a miſerable creature, a poor fragment of humanity, an imbecile drone, more falſe to his divine calling than the verieſt drudge whom he looks down upon with profound contempt. Men of leiſure, in the beſt inſtances, teach the worth of labor quite as much as the men of work; for what greater proof is there of the need of uſeful occupation than the lives of the moſt earneſt men here and in Europe, whom wealth or ſtation exempts from common toil only to open ſtill more ſtirring fields of enterpriſe and uſefulneſs. Even the lives of titled nobles preſent to us the worth of induſtry and the folly of all manner of idle vagrancy, whether the vagrancy that loiters the ſtreets in rags or that which daſhes along the pavement in jewels, both extremes ſlighting faithful effort, and demanding indulgence without any return by fidelity. Honor to every man who accepts cheerfully his work in time, and ſerves God and his neighbor by bringing ſomething uſeful to paſs—no matter whether he plants ſeed in the expectation of the harvest—trains thought for efficient action—or ſets any worthy plan upon the way to its end. The hours bleſs him as they paſs by, calling out the good that is in his nature, and bringing to him ſome meaſure of the good of Providence.

Yet we are not to work always, and even when we are at work, we learn that many things do not follow our bidding, and we muſt wait upon theirs. More and more we learn this truth as years interpret to us our own limitation and the force of the great tide upon which we and all things float. Our patience is quite as much a meaſure of our wiſdom as our enterpriſe: nay, what folly ſtamps every enterpriſe which is not begun in the patience that can bear delays as well as in the courage that can dare riſks. Children of time, when we are doing our beſt we muſt wait God's hours for opportunity in our eſpecial aims, and above all our eſpecial aims we muſt lean upon him to carry us forward in the one divine way, which earthly power may accept but not control. Bleſſed is the office of true patience in relation to time. Vaſt is the loſs it ſhuns by keeping for efficient action the time and thought ſaved from fretting and ſtruggling againſt what cannot be helped. Vaſt is the gain it ſecures by keeping the ſoul calm before God, accepting the allotments of his providence, and watching wiſely the leſſons of the events which it cannot control. Are there not twelve hours in the day, ſaid he who conſecrated them alike by his waiting and his work

—whofe crowning facrifice, alike in its act and its fufferance, illuftrated the worth of time, and leaves upon its track the alternate footprints of labor and patience to mark the way of eternal life. Bleffed are the hours to us, when calmed by his patience as well as quickened by his fidelity.

Prefenting thus the twofold afpect of our duty in relation to time, we pafs on to confider the method that can rightly adjuft the two elements, active and paffive. What can be more practical than the question—How fhall we beft divide the hours between working and waiting, or labor and reft? There is no numerical rule that can apply to all, for the power of exertion and the need of repofe differ widely with different conftitutions and modes of life. But a general principle may be at once ftated which can be applied to every cafe. We may juftly fay that is the true method of dividing the hours which provides beft for the duties of our pofition, and keeps in moft healthful balance the powers of our nature. Let each one confider this principle for himfelf, for each day, and for the general order of life.

What have we to do to meet fairly the demands of our pofition, and how shall we find time for thefe demands? The order, which is heaven's firſt law, will be found to be a wonderful regulator of the hours that are marked by heaven's own light. True, indeed, it is that we cannot wholly command our time, and much of every active man's day is at the mercy of circumſtances beyond his control. This very fact, inſtead of diſparaging method, ſhould confirm it, for a wiſe man will make fair allowance for all the expoſures of his poſition, and whilſt keeping himſelf ready for cares that come without his bidding, he will find due time alſo for duties that wait his attention. Let every one of us have a plan for the day, ſtrict enough to bring every duty to a ſpecific point, and flexible enough to allow of adjuſtment to circumſtances—free alike, in ſhort, from flighty laxity and ſlaviſh punctilio. Frame ſuch a plan wiſely, with the aid of the beſt examples, and in view of our own condition, do we not find that we have made a great diſcovery, and the hours often ſcorned as ſo ſhort and fleeting open to us powers and opportunities beyond which no gold can purchaſe.

The true method will not only meet our perſonal duties, but will alſo keep our powers in due and healthful balance. In one reſpect we may underſtand this balance well enough, and the moraliſt need not inſiſt upon the need of a juſt proportion between the ſleeping and the waking hours, although in city life even this juſt balance is ſometimes loſt, and people fooliſhly ſpoil the day's energy by midnight diſſipation. But the balance of waking and ſleeping is to a thoughtful man but the loweſt form of a balance that ſhould adjuſt the whole life. As we once read in the great work of Schubert on the ſoul, it is but a part of that polarity or harmony of contraſts which has its higheſt manifeſtation in the true ſpiritual life that goes forth in filial obedience and returns to refreſh itſelf in filial truſt, in ſhort, in work and in faith, or in labor and in prayer. Without purſuing this theme into its higheſt ſpiritual ſpheres, conſider the balance of our nature under the obvious and practical relation of toil and recreation, or work-time and paſtime. No man uſes time well, or follows God's manifeſt law, who ſlights either of theſe elements. Without toil a man is a mere drone—without recreation he is a mere drudge. We work more efficiently for ſome play, and we play more cheerfully for ſome work. There are few ſubjects more important to the health of the beſt minds, and to the very virtue of the nations, than this ſame problem of the balance of work and play. God himſelf bids us ſeriouſly conſider it, and it will be found that the very laws of our being urge it upon our thought. It is almoſt as great a matter to know how to play as to know how to work: in fact, the nature of our work decides the proper character of our play. The guiding principle is this: that a man's beſt recreation conſiſts not in idleneſs, for this beyond a certain limit is an intolerable burden, and has compelled far more men to ſelf-deſtruction than hard work; but his beſt recreation conſiſts in ſuch action as reſts the faculties that have been overtaſked, and calls out the faculties that have been dormant. Children underſtand or rather practiſe the true principle better than we men, who are ſo apt to halt between drudging and droning. Children let looſe from ſchool, refreſh themſelves by letting looſe the buoyant faculties ſo long reſtrained over their taſks, and kind nature through their cheerful play develops their frames, quickens their ſenſes, and refreſhes their ſpirits. Where is the man who carries out the ſame principle through life, and does by his reaſon what childhood does by inſtinct—the man who carries through his whole life a method of recreation that balances his routine of toil? This idea would make ſociety generally far more genial, and would give life a far larger range. There would be fairer allowance for what is generally called amuſement by the public, and each man would decide upon his own amuſement in ſuch a way as beſt to refreſh and to quicken his powers. The great law of alternation would be heeded, and many would find that change of purſuit is to them the beſt play. When the eye is dazzled by the yellow ſplendor of ſome gilded pageant, it is refreſhed not by cloſing itſelf, but by reſting upon the blue ſky; and when inflamed by the glare of the reddening ſun, it is refreſhed by turning to the green of the pleaſant paſtures. The whole being partakes of this ſame law, and every faculty like the eye demands in its own way a change, like that of the eye from yellow to blue, or from red to green. Imaginative men, weary with viſions, refreſh themſelves with matters of fact, like Dante who ſought recreation in the exact reaſonings of Ariſtotle, or like Goethe, who went from his books to the fields, and found playfellows in the flowers. Men of ſcientific reſearch find their refreſhment in the play of the imaginative faculties, like Galileo, who rejoiced in muſic, or like Kepler, who leaped ever from the laws of matter to the harmonies which they fuggeft. Men of abftraction find their play in things concrete, like Leibnitz, who amufed himfelf with experimenting upon carriages, or Locke, who bufied himfelf with the printing art. Statefmen, bufy with men and nations, love the folace of nature, and, like Cicero, and almoft all kindred minds, delight in the farm and the garden. Wife is the man who fo choofes his play that it refts his mind, refrefhes his fpirits, enlarges his culture, and fends him back a heartier worker to the regular labor of his fphere. He will in fome way divide his time between what the ancients called mathematics and mufic, meaning by mathematics whatever tafks the intellect, and by mufic whatever fets the faculties into free play without any tafking. The majeftic name of Jefus is not defecrated by affociation with this idea. He who afked, Are there not twelve hours of the day? did not frown on the play of childhood, nor the recreations of men. The very fpirit in which he faid to his weary difciples, "Sleep on now and take your reft," was developed in that facred, yet genial Chriftian life, which checked the heathen revel only to cheer with a new fong the hearts of men—which emptied the Colifeum of its murderers and heroes to prepare the way for a purer, brighter, focial order, which fhall blend wifely labor and recreation —when the hours fhall follow the path which the Mafter has opened, and, in recurrent work and play, as with alternate feet, fhall move their appointed round. Life will then have its profe fide and its poetic fide, not hoftile but ever coming nearer harmony—our profy work the braver becaufe of the poetic fong and vifion, the poetic play the more true and joyous becaufe of the profaic thought and enterprife.

Thus wifely balanced, the hours not only lead us to our earthly work and reft, but interpret to us eternity, by giving us a larger and clearer fenfe of things immutable as we pafs through the changes of time. Wifely has the civilized world changed the computation of time fince Jefus came. In many things the gofpel made a new era, but in nothing more decidedly than in opening eternity into time. Bleffed be the Chriftian Hours, not fleeting, not fad, not groaning a perpetual dirge over decay and death—but ever opening new blefs-ings, teaching deeper truths, infpiring purer affec-tions, urging diviner ufes, leading the foul ever nearer God, ever further into the life eternal.

XIII.

STUDY IN THE COUNTRY.

A VACATION LETTER.

Dear ——, If you and I had the whole world before us, and were on the look-out for the beſt of all places for earneſt thought and faithful ſtudy, it might be a ſerious queſtion whether our choice would fall upon the city, with all its ſocial incentives, or the country, with its meditative quiet. Happy are we, however, in combining ſome of the advantages of both places, and in ſtealing away for a ſhort ſeaſon into ſome rural ſhade. It is clear to me that the city gives moſt ſpur to the thought that labors for the preſent hour, whilſt the country is moſt favorable to retroſpective ſtudies and proſpective viſions. One needs a quicker pulſe than ſtirs in theſe quiet villages to move him to think, and write, and work fitly for the electric temper of the buſy world, which makes ſo much of To-day and ſo little of Yesterday and To-morrow. The city indeed is full of the footprints of former generations, and every old building and book-shop is a chronicle of years gone by, at once jogging memory and anticipation. Yet whatever impression is made is too soon trodden down by the great throng; whatever spark of electricity is communicated is too soon discharged, where isolation is so difficult, and nonconductors are nonentities. Happy would he be who could use the city like a seedsman's store, and bear away the precious grains to calmer and more congenial soil. Happy he who could know Rome, and think and write in Tusculum, instead of being pent for so many months within brick walls.

When we first came here, a few weeks ago, the very air and sky seemed to challenge me to be their playfellow. The flitting clouds and the rippling waters seemed like the old companions of youth calling me back to them, and it was pleasant indeed to find in nature and in books so much countenance for this frolicsome mood. But the kind mother whose training we can never escape understands us well, and allows us to play that we may learn to be more sober and more industrious. Her pleasant face has given some intimations already of her ſerious purpoſe, and her merry voice once in a while deepens into a ſolemn tone. Laſt night, after a day of moſt delicious, dreamy beauty, the evening ſky put on a mantle of deep and ſombre red, as if the refulgent ſummer would give us a hint of the ſober autumn, and bid us uſe the golden hours to ſtore up precious fruits for the time of the falling leaf.

As we ſtood before an opening between over-arching trees, the weſtern ſky was a gorgeous and ſolemn cathedral window, and its glowing cryſtal was painted with the ſweet landſcape ſo boldly projected againſt the horizon. There in the back-ground of the picture ſtood Greenfield Hill, that height not unknown to fame, with its graceful church-ſpire and its rural cemetery; there, too, was our little grove of cheſtnuts and cedars, with cot-tage and ruſtic arbor on either ſide. The hour ſeemed ſacred to memory, and the looker-on might expect to hear that elder Madonna, Nature, herſelf chant a veſper hymn full of elegiac tenderneſs over them who ſleep under thoſe white tombſtones, and over all her loſt children, and refute the ſkeptic's ſcandal, that the univerſal mother cares not for the faireſt of her offspring when they are gone, and laughs over their graves as merrily as over ſpring daiſies. Like Mary at the ſepulchre, if they who know her beſt can tell, ſhe mourns at times for her elect of the buried generations.

The ſea, too, in whoſe calm waters we daily bathe, and our little girls frolic without fear, as if it were harmleſs as domeſtic Croton, once in a while changes its aſpect and voice. A few nights ago we could hear from our cottage door the daſh of its great waves, with the moan of their retreat. The evening breeze, laden with ſuch ſounds, ſtirred many a grave thought, and I could not but think of the ſtory which theſe uſually quiet waters would tell if their ſecrets could be known. One awful night there was, when, in ſight of theſe hills, hundreds of lives were floating to deſtruction in a ſhip of fire upon a ſea of ice; among them that mild and heroic man from whom ſo many of us learned the language that has unlocked ſo many treaſures, and which has been lately the key to ſo much pleaſure and profit here. I have thought of Follen always tenderly and gratefully, but never more ſo than now; and theſe twenty years ſince leaving his tuition ſeem but a day.

I will follow the vein of reverie thus invited, by

giving a paſſing ſketch of an author upon whom I chanced to light, and of whom, perhaps, our readers may be as ignorant as I was before vacation.

I have been at work for a week or two upon a ſubject connected with the new Jewiſh Literature; and from a chip that has fallen from the work-bench I may perhaps whittle out ſomething worth looking at, if not very pretty. Full autumn, with its ſere leaves and ruſſet tints, might ſeem the beſt accompaniment to the ſtudy of a mind ſo retro-ſpective, ſo loſt in memory as the Jewiſh, yet I pro-miſe to ſay nothing too ſad or too heavy for ſum-mer reading, even if I could.

A HEBREW POET BROUGHT TO LIGHT.

Going from our Proteſtant age, and excepting the ſeedtime of primitive Chriſtianity, no period of Chriſtendom has for us more intereſt than the eleventh and twelfth centuries, with the few years before and after. Then the Papacy conſolidated its doctrines and policy, and bade fair to ſubdue the whole world to itſelf. Art and ſcience ſeemed to become its vaſſals, and the riſe of a new and wonderful architecture, and the prevalence of a daring yet obedient philoſophy, indicated that reaſon and imagination were willing to kneel before the transformed wafer as the preſence of God, and before its ghoſtly guardians as the vicegerents of Heaven. The Norman Conqueſt and the Cruſades were but ſuperficial ſigns of the deep-ſeated fire that was burning in the heart of Chriſtendom. In its heat the ſtubborn elements of hoſtile nationalities were fuſed, and from the flowing lava our modern languages came. The majeſtic Roman was won from its ſtatelineſs; and before melting into Italian sweetneſs, it exchanged its claſſic verſe for the Romantic rhyme, and in the hymns of the Church left the Virgilian meaſure for that recurrent chime which is the lyric dance of devotion, as if grave Numa himſelf had caught the new enthuſiaſm, and moved with choral ſteps to the ſound of harp and cymbal before the Ark. One who has been bred among our modern diſſent and individualiſm is aſtoniſhed at the almoſt univerſal acquiescence in the reigning absolutism. The Albigenses and their kindred Proteſtant confeſſors were not ſilent, but their fate illuſtrates the power of the prieſthood which they arraigned, and the ſword and firebrand of De Montfort were the anſwer of the Church to her refractory children. Brave voices like Arnold's of Brefcia, were heard only to be filenced at the flaming ftake, and the martyr's afhes, caft into the Tiber, were not allowed to reft even with kindred duft. Philofophy had not blinded her eyes, yet was quite willing to invoke the fame ghoftly protection for her rival theories; and Abelard the Rationalift, and Bernard the champion of Orthodoxy, much as they differed in metaphyfics, were willing to fanction the fame awful ritual, and own the real prefence in the fame morfel of bread.

Yet the mind of our whole race was not then Roman Catholic, and never has been, and never will be. South of Chriftendom, the great race that fpoke the Arabic language and held to the Crefcent, extended from Jerufalem to Spain, and protefted againft Rome, not with the fword alone, for their fcholars and metaphyficians had given them other arguments for Monotheifm even than the Koran. The palmy days of the Caliphate indeed had paffed, yet Arabic learning had its ripeft fruits ftill treafured up, and the refiftance which the Crufaders met at Jerufalem came from a force not wholly brutal nor fuperftitious. It was at the City of David that the two leading powers of the earth came into conflict, and we are left to judge of the merits and the iſſue of the ſtrife by the teſtimony of one party alone. The Saracen had his ſtory to tell, and we ſhould like to liſten to his tale. But at the other end of Chriſtendom the ſame antagoniſm appeared. In Spain, Arabia and Rome met in battle. Caſtile was on the border of the arena, and this little book, that has beguiled ſome of theſe ſummer hours, has much of its intereſt from the fact that it allows us to look upon the rival faiths through the eyes of a gifted man of that race of Abraham that claims to have given a religion to both antagoniſts, and from both to have received cruel wrong. It is called Divan des Castiliers Abu'l-Hassan Juda ha-Levi. Von Abraham Geiger. Breslau. 1851.

With the poems that conſtitute this Divan of the Caſtilian Jew, Juda ha-Levi, biographical ſketches and notes are given that throw much light upon the poet and his times. Whatever period of his life we chooſe to ſtudy, we find the ſame eſſential characteriſtics in different ſtages of development. It is the Hebrew poet ſtill, the ſame impaſſioned, ſenſuous, devout, yearning nature, whether in his early love-ſongs, his later philoſophizing, or the religious poems of his mature and declining years.

The Hebrew pietiſm was the leaven that worked in his inmoſt life; and when his buoyant muſe dealt in merry riddles and gay ſerenades, it loved more to find themes in the cheerful feſtivals of the ſynagogue, and ſing of ſome bridal which the nation could bleſs in the name of the old law, and with the hope that waited for Iſrael's Conſolation. He ſtudied medicine, the only profeſſion except the rabbinical that was open to his race; and diſtaſte for its practice, combined with unſucceſsful love for his fair couſin, gave a melancholy tinge to his compoſition, which appears in the many poems of friendſhip, apparently on the verge of manhood, in ſomething of that ſweet, ſad ſentiment which Goethe has ſo powerfully brought out in the character of Taſso. Then the ſenſe of his high calling, a paſſion to be ſomething and do ſomething for his oppreſſed nation, roſe within him; verſe ſeemed to him but a trifling with words, and he rebuked the new ſchool of Hebrew bards that had been forming ſince the ſeventh century, and repented that he had encouraged the taſte for rhymed ſtanzas, or any innovation upon the ſimple, ſolemn ſtrain of the old pſalmiſts and prophets. Yet nature and the age was too ſtrong for his ſevere taſte, and we ſoon find his muſe again moving to the march of the borrowed Arabic meaſure, and ſhowing that a new day had come to the Jewiſh Zion as well as the Roman Parnaſſus. His poems take a deeper tone and higher range, mingling a myſtical devotion with a reſtleſs longing for Jeruſalem. He carries the ſame ſpirit into philoſophy; and in a work in the Arabic language he embodied his philoſophy of religion under the fictitious form of a dialogue at the court of the King of Khazar, held between the King, a Mohammedan, a Chriſtian, and a Jewiſh rabbi. The argument of courſe is with the rabbi, and the king, according to an hiſtorical fact as well as this philoſophical fiction, becomes a convert to the synagogue, inſtead of following his Turcoman compeers to the moſque. This book was, ſoon after Juda's death, tranſlated into Hebrew, and afterwards into Latin, Spaniſh, and German, and editions have been often publiſhed, the laſt at Leipſic in 1842. The philoſopher does not wholly lay aſide the poet, but baſes all truth and all religion upon the Spirit of God in the ſoul, beſtowed in ſuch fulneſs upon the choſen people. Inſtead of undertaking to legitimate religion by philoſophy, he legitimates philoſophy by religion, and ſtarts with faith as the primal and effential fact of wifdom. The calling of Abraham and his pofterity gives him his connecting bridge between the abftract and concrete, the fubjective and objective, fo that he reafons for the authority of Ifrael very much as Bernard or Aquinas reafoned for the fovereignty of Rome. With the Romifh zealots, too, he agreed in the paffion for Jerufalem; and the hero of his philofophical fiction, at the clofe of his victorious dialogue, announces his determination to go to the Holy Land, and abides by it in fpite of all the fears and promifes held out to him. It was but Juda himfelf who borrowed the garb of the rabbin to fpeak his own conviction and his own yearning. He folemnly refolved to fee with his own eyes the hills and waters of Zion. About the year 1140, when about fixty years of age, and not far from the time when Bernard's ghoftly voice was to fummon a new army of the crofs to repeat the Crufade, the Caftilian poet and philofopher turned his face towards Jerufalem with all of a Crufader's zeal in his heart, but with far other weapons in his hands. On his way by the fouthern route through Spain, the Mediterranean, and Egypt, he was welcomed as a prince among the chiefs and communities of the faithful, and gratulatory poems were interchanged between himſelf and the leading poets of the age. At Egypt, where the Jews enjoyed ſuch religious liberty, and where the brilliant genius of Maimonides was to reward the kindneſs of the court that protected him with ſuch reflected honor, Juda was almoſt forced by friendly conſtraint to give up his pilgrimage, and to exchange his dream of Jeruſalem, now in hoſtile hands, for Egypt, more rich, it was ſaid, in ancient remembrance, and ſo favored with kings now more merciful than the Pharaohs. But the poet was inflexible, and tore himſelf away from the charmed circle of learned friends to wander alone in the land trodden by David. His wiſh was probably granted, and he touched the ſacred ſoil, although two ſhort poems are all that ſpeak of him after he reached the Tyrian coaſt. He is ſuppoſed to have died ſoon after, illuſtrating the lot of ſo many lives that are devoted to ſome fond hope, and who chaſe it inceſſantly, and find their reward more in the chaſe than in the goal. It is dangerous to dream of any earthly ſpot or fortune as the heaven of our ſoul, and to a mind like Juda's, Paleſtine itſelf might not fulfil all the viſions of his fancy. Whether ſome violent hand was laid upon him among the heterogeneous and reftlefs population there, or his ftrength yielded under the exhauftion of travel, no fure record tells. We may reafonably believe that he died among the fcenes that had fo long haunted his imagination, and that in death he found fpeaking emblems around him of a heavenly Jerufalem which no violence can lay wafte. His famous fong of Zion, compofed before leaving Caftile, might have been fit requiem for him, for in that glowing lyric he celebrated God's mercy to that land of promife, conjured before him its faints and fages, found food for the foul in its very air, fragrance in its very duft, and rejoiced in the vifion of its returning glory and its renewed youth.

The fpirit that led him hither to die was no vain illufion, for it has paffed into the poems that have founded his fame and perpetuated his influence. In the original Hebrew they have been introduced into the fervice-books of the fynagogues, and of late have been tranflated into the tongues of other nations. The Hebrew Platonist, Moses Mendelssohn, from his own fellow-feeling, gave a German drefs to fome of his mafterpieces, and Herder's univerfal literary fympathy placed him in his collection of bards. But to Profeſſor Luzzato, of Padua, we are indebted for the only full edition of his Divan, which was printed in Prague, 1846, from a manuſcript found in Tunis, and conſiſting of the original collection firſt made, ſhortly after Juda's death, in 1154. Geiger, a celebrated Hebrew ſcholar and author, has followed the edition of Luzzato, and in German given the modern world for the firſt time a fair idea of the Caſtilian poet.

So is it that that which is hid comes to light; and no earneſt word is likely to be ſpoken in vain. The book, the bookſeller ſays, is quite a favorite among the Jews in this country, and here in the New World the poet's nation renew his yearnings for the old Fatherland. Here in the buſh we have read this volume, and we now cloſe its pretty paper covers, thinking that the human race is meant to be a ſomewhat more comprehenſive fraternity than bigots dream, and that Providence may have ſome work for the Jew to do before the curtain falls and time ceaſes.

THE END.

JAMES MILLER,

Successor to C. S. FRANCIS & CO.,

554 BROADWAY, NEW YORK,

HAS RECENTLY PUBLISHED

PALEY'S EVIDENCES OF CHRISTIANITY,

WITH ANNOTATIONS BY ARCHBISHOP WHATELY.

One Volume octavo. *Cloth*, $1.75; *half calf*, $3.00; *full calf*, $3.75.

The Publisher begs respectfully to call the attention of the religious and thinking portion of the community to his very handsome edition of "**A View of the Evidences of Christianity,**" the work of the celebrated **Paley**, a man remarkable for vigor and clearness of intellect, and originality of character, and acknowledged by all to be the greatest among the divines of his age, and without a superior since the days of the early fathers of the Protestant Church.

BACON'S ESSAYS,

WITH ANNOTATIONS BY ARCHBISHOP WHATELY.

Fourth Edition.

With considerable Additions and Corrections.

One Vol. 8vo. *Cloth*, $2.00; *half calf*, $3.25; *full calf*, $4.00.

A GUIDE TO THE KNOWLEDGE OF LIFE,

VEGETABLE AND ANIMAL.

Being a Comprehensive Ma ual of Physiology, viewed in Relation to the Maintenance of Health.

BY ROBERT JAMES MANN, M.D.

88 *Cents.*

"This book is by one of the scientific teachers of the time; sound in knowledge, earnest in purpose, and above all writers on intricate subjects, gifted with wonderful powers of explanation and description."—*Chambers' Journal.*

JAMES MILLER,

Successor to C. S. FRANCIS & CO.,

Bookseller, Publisher, and Importer,

554 BROADWAY, NEW YORK,

Has for sale a very complete and extensive Stock of

ENGLISH AND AMERICAN BOOKS,

IN THE VARIOUS DEPARTMENTS OF LITERATURE:

INCLUDING

STANDARD EDITIONS OF THE BEST AUTHORS IN

HISTORY, BIOGRAPHY, BELLES-LETTRES, &c.,

FINELY BOUND IN MOROCCO, CALF, ETC., FOR

DRAWING-ROOM LIBRARIES;

LIKEWISE ORNAMENTED AND RICHLY EMBELLISHED BOOKS OF PLATES FOR THE CENTRE-TABLE.

☞ *Particular attention given to orders from Public and Private Libraries.*

ENGLISH AND AMERICAN PERIODICALS

supplied, and served carefully and faithfully to Subscribers throughout the city, or sent by mail to the country. Orders from any part of the world, with a remittance or reference for payment in New York, will be promptly attended to.

IMPORTATION OF ALL BOOKS AND PERIODICALS

for which he may receive orders, a small commission only being charged for the business. The same attention given to an order for a single copy as for a quantity.

Prose Writers of Germany.

BY FREDERICK H. HEDGE, D. D.

Illustrated with an engraved Title-page from a design by Leutze; and portraits of Goethe, Luther, Lessing, Mendelssohn, Herder, Schiller, Richter, and Schlegel. Complete in one volume octavo.

Cloth, $3.00; gilt, $3.50; antique morocco, $5.00.

Contents.

LUTHER,	HAMANN,	GOETHE,	ZSCHOKKE,
BOEHME,	WIELAND,	SCHILLER,	F. SCHLEGEL,
SANCTA CLARA,	MUSAUS,	FICHTE,	HARDENBERG,
MOSER,	CLAUDIUS,	RICHTER,	TIECK,
KANT,	LAVATER,	A. W. SCHLEGEL,	SCHELLING,
LESSING,	JACOBI,	SCHLEIERMACHER,	HOFFMANN,
MENDELSSOHN,	HERDER,	HEGEL,	CHAMISSO.

This work comprises a list of the most eminent writers of Germany, together with copious extracts from their works, beginning with LUTHER and reaching up to the present time. For those who are interested in the literature of Germany, it presents a valuable aid in becoming more intimately acquainted with the German mind: and to the curious an excitement which will grow stronger as their taste is cultivated.

We find here valuable extracts, given from their prose writings. Al though the writers follow in chronological order, and LUTHER stands at the head of his intellectual brethren, the longest space is allowed to those who claim our greatest attention; and GOETHE therefore occupies the most conspicuous position both in the specimens given and the selection of the pieces. Next to GOETHE, SCHILLER appears in an article upon Naïve and Sentimental Poetry. Then we have LESSING, the first critic of his time. Next to him comes HERDER, a devout philosopher, and a clear-sighted intellect. The two brothers SCHLEGEL—William, the noble interpreter and translator of Shakspeare, and Frederic, known best by his investigations of the language and wisdom of the Indians—follow him, and MOSES MENDELSSOHN, a Jewish philosopher, closes the series of these writers.

"The author of this work—for it is well entitled to the name of an original production, though mainly consisting of translations—Rev. Dr. Hedge, of Providence, is qualified, as few men are in this country, or wherever the English language is written, for the successful accomplishment of the great literary enterprise to which he has devoted his leisure for several years."

"We venture to say that there cannot be crowded into the same compass a more faithful representation of the German mind, or a richer exhibition of the profound thought, subtle speculation, massive learning and genial temper, that characterize the most eminent literary men of that nation."—*Harbinger.*

"What excellent matter we here have. The choicest gems of exuberant fancy the most polished productions of scholarship, the richest flow of the heart, the deepest lessons of wisdom, all translated so well by Mr. Hedge and his friends, that they seem to have been first written by masters of the English tongue."

"We have read the book with rare pleasure, and have derived not less information than enjoyment."—*Knickerbocker.*

Pycroft's Course of English Reading.

A Course of English Reading, adapted to every taste and capacity. By Rev. James Pycroft, of Trinity College, Oxford. Edited with alterations, emendations, and additions, by J. A. Spencer, D.D.

Extract from the Preface.

"Miss Jane C. divided her in-door hours into three parts; the housekeeping and dinner-ordering cares of life claimed one part; hearing two younger sisters say their lessons, a second part; and during the third, and most delightful remainder, she would lock her chamber door, and move on the marker of Russell's 'Modern Europe,' at the rate of never less than fifteen pages an hour, and sometimes more.

"Being so vexatious as to ask wherein her satisfaction consisted, I was told, in the thought that she did her duty; that she kept her resolution; that she read as much as her friends; that continually fewer histories remained to be read; and that she hoped one day to excel in literature.

"A few torturing questions elicited that neither the labor nor the resolution aforesaid, had produced any sensible increase, or more than a vague but anxious expectation, of available information or mental improvement. A painful suspicion arose that there was some truth in the annoying remark of a certain idle companion, that she was 'stupefying her brains for no good.'

"The exposure of an innocent delusion is mere cruelty, unless you replace the shadow by the substance; so, a list of books and plan of operations was promised by the next post. Adam Smith attempted in a pamphlet what resulted in his Wealth of Nations, after the labor of thirty years. My letter grew into a volume now offered for the guidance of youth in each and every department of literature.

"Without aspiring to direct the future studies of men, Macaulay in History, of Dr. Buckland in Geology, or of the Duke of Wellington in military tactics, he is happy to say, that very learned men have expressed their regret that in their early studies they had not the benefit of such simple guidance as this volume affords."

"A volume which we can conscientiously recommend as marking out an accurate course of historical and general reading, from which a vast acquisition of sound knowledge must result. The arrangement and system are no less admirable than the selection of authors pointed out for study."—*Literary Gazette.*

"An admirable little work, intended to suggest various ways in which the acquisition of knowledge through the medium of books, may be adapted to the leisure time and taste of those who would educate themselves. The plain terms in which the latter consideration is urged has something in them decidedly original; and especially would we commend Mr. Pycroft to the notice of those who feel at times overwhelmed by the heaped up piles of learning that beset the hesitating student."—*Albion.*

"We say unhesitatingly that this is a most excellent work, which should be in the hands of every student and reader of the English language; and we have to thank Dr. Spencer for the valuable additions he has made to it, admirably adapting it to American wants. Whoever will follow the advice it contains for one or two hours a day will soon acquire such habits of reflection, and so much general knowledge as will much increase the pleasure of both their solitary and social hours."—*Albany Spectator.*

www.ingramcontent.com/pod-product-compliance
Lightning Source LLC
LaVergne TN
LVHW021359110826
845150LV00007B/1713

* 9 7 8 1 4 2 5 5 1 3 0 8 5 *